CONFECTIONERY
SCHOOL

CONFECTIONERY
SCHOOL

Nougats, caramels, truffles, candy canes, toffee,
marshmallows, fudge, pralines, lollipops...
90 step-by-step recipes

GRUB STREET • LONDON

FOREWORD

With *Confectionery School*, Le Cordon Bleu opens up a new culinary world. This book provides you with our Chefs' know-how and recipes so that you can make your own confectionery. Mirroring the way in which our students learn, this book contains illustrated chapters on various aspects of the craft of confectionery, including tempering, moulding and coating chocolate, as well as cooking, colouring, shaping and decorating with sugar, enabling you to gradually improve your skills.

From pink pralines to soft caramels, bergamotes de Nancy to nougatines de Nevers, from lokum to turrón, you'll learn how to make a range of traditional and modern confectionery, and acquire new professional techniques from France and beyond. Discover a vibrant world of gourmet flavours and textures.

Le Cordon Bleu is the leading global network of culinary arts and hospitality management institutes. With over 125 years of teaching experience, the institute offers a wide range of diploma programmes, from vocational certificates to university diplomas that specialise in gastronomy, hospitality and tourism. Accredited in more than 20 countries, Le Cordon Bleu trains nearly 20,000 students who represent over 100 nationalities each year in cuisine, pastry and boulangerie as well as in wine and hospitality management.

Through our institutes and partner universities, Le Cordon Bleu has created quality curricula to support students in their career choices. Le Cordon Bleu students excel in a diverse range of careers, going on to become journalists, food critics, sommeliers, wine agents, writers, food photographers, restaurant managers, nutritionists, chefs and/or entrepreneurs.

The success of many of our graduates is a testament to the quality of our teaching, from Julia Child to Yotam Ottolenghi. Many of our former students have been honoured with prestigious titles and awards, such as Garima Arora, Clara Puig, Cristóbal Muñoz and Darren Chin, who have been awarded a Michelin star. Past Le Cordon Bleu alumni, such as Luciana Berry, Jessica Wang and many others, have also won culinary competitions such as Top Chef and MasterChef. Our alumni also include successful entrepreneurs like Virgilio Martínez and Pía León (named Best Female Chef in the World by the World's 50 Best Restaurants in 2023), whose restaurant Central was ranked number one by the World's 50 Best Restaurants. Le Cordon Bleu is proud to see the professional recognition its alumni garner around the world.

Le Cordon Bleu, which has always remained true to its philosophy of striving for excellence, offers an exceptional educational environment in the world's capitals of gastronomy. Proof of this is the fact that, in 2022, Le Cordon Bleu was awarded the prize for Best Culinary Training Establishment in Europe and Best Culinary Training Establishment in the World by the World Culinary Awards. Taught by Chefs who have worked in the best establishments and who are experts in the world of gastronomy, Le Cordon Bleu's training is recognised worldwide.

Le Cordon Bleu's programmes also place great emphasis on pedagogical innovation. Indeed, over the years, the institute has witnessed how the culinary arts and the hospitality industry have evolved, and its new programmes are the fruit of this observation. The new programmes offered by our institutes address today's keen interest in nutrition, well-being, vegetarian cuisine, food science and social and environmental responsibility, and illustrate the changes taking place in the world of gastronomy.

Being a driving force for change is nothing new for Le Cordon Bleu. Journalist Marthe Distel, who founded Le Cordon Bleu in 1895, had the pioneering vision of offering culinary training to everyone, especially women. Open to a non-professional public, Le Cordon Bleu began teaching the techniques used by the great masters of French cuisine, which proved to be hugely successful. Both women and an international clientele flocked to the school – the first Russian student was welcomed in 1897, and the first Japanese student enrolled in 1905. By 1914, Le Cordon Bleu had four schools in Paris and had succeeded in its commitment to innovation.

Today, Le Cordon Bleu's mission is to promote gastronomy by highlighting quality models in the culinary arts and the hospitality industry. Le Cordon Bleu instils international standards as well as respect for local tastes and customs, and puts French culinary techniques at the service of the cuisines of the world. Amongst the programmes offered by the institute, some at the request of the Ministries of Education of various countries, are courses on Peruvian, Brazilian, Mexican, Spanish, Japanese and Thai cuisines. Le Cordon Bleu also takes part in many events celebrating culture, know-how, flavours and ingredients from around the world, working with embassies, local governments and various organisations, as well as international trade fairs and competitions.

Le Cordon Bleu regularly publishes books, many of which have received international acclaim: some have become benchmarks in culinary training, and over 14 million books have been sold worldwide. Thanks to the advice and techniques of our Chefs, these books are our way of encouraging gastronomy enthusiasts of all levels to take the plunge.

I hope that *Confectionery School* will help you to appreciate the ingenuity of confectioners, who, using simple ingredients, have succeeded in creating confectionery that is as aesthetically pleasing as it is delicious. It is an invitation to share, a small token of affection, a delicious treat and a source of gourmet pleasure that will bring a smile to your face. Enjoy your discovery!

Amitiés gourmandes

ANDRÉ COINTREAU

President of Le Cordon Bleu International

CONTENTS

The Art of Confectionery 13
Le Cordon Bleu key dates 14
Le Cordon Bleu institutes around the world 19

CONFECTIONERY TECHNIQUES 22
The ingredients used in confectionery 24
Confectionery equipment 30
Cooking sugar 32
Candying: Candied orange peel 36
Strawberry flavoured syrup 38
Candy syrup 39
Fondant 40
Almond paste 42

Starch tray 43
Praline paste 44
Tempering chocolate over a bain-marie 45
Tempering chocolate by seeding 46
Tempering chocolate with Mycryo® 47
Tempering chocolate by tabling on marble 48
Checking the chocolate is tempered 50
Coating chocolates 51
Moulding chocolates 52
Making paper cones for decorating 54
Decorating chocolates 55
Making chocolate Easter fish 57

CONFECTIONERY CLASSICS 58

Mandarin fruit jellies 60

Liquorice 64

Ravioli sweets filled with fruit jelly 66

Pink marshmallows 70

Soft nougat 74

Hard nougat 78

Chocolate spread 82

Chewy caramels with fine "fleur de sel" sea salt 86

Hard coffee caramels 90

Candy canes 94

Crystallised rose petals and crystallised violets 96

Filled barley sugar 98

Liquid-centred sweets 102

Confit chestnuts and candied chestnuts 106

Chocolate-coated candied orange peel 110

Mendiants and chocolate buttons with hundreds and thousands 112

Chocolate-coated almonds 114

Chocolate nougat 116

Dark and milk chocolate truffles 120

Chocolate praline rochers and white chocolate coconut rochers 124

Gold-flecked palettes 128

Moulded passion fruit chocolates 132

Griottines® chocolates and chocolate fondant cherries 134

Filled chocolate lollipops 138

REGIONAL CONFECTIONERY 142

Calissons 144

Pink pralines 148

Bergamotes from Nancy
   and fizzy berlingots 152

Apple sweets 156

Mirabelles from Lorraine 158

Nougatines de Nevers 164

Coussins de Lyon 168

Caprices 172

Menhirs 176

Tas de sel 180

Dark chocolate sarments 182

Ardoises 184

INTERNATIONAL CONFECTIONERY 188

Orange marmalade 190

Lokums 192

Wine gums 194

Tamarind and coconut lollipops 198

Vanilla fudge and coffee toffee 202

Butterscotch 206

Dalgona 208

Chikki 212

Stuffed dates 214

Turrón 218

Halva 219

Cremino 220

Gianduja and gianduiotto 224

Mozartkugel 228

Schokoküss 232

Brigadeiro 236

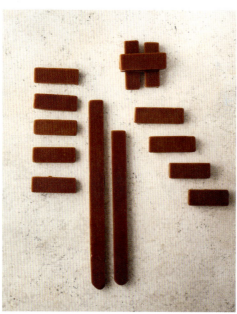

MODERN CONFECTIONERY ... 238

Pressed fruit bars ... 240
Pears candied in birch sugar ... 244
Reduced sugar raspberry jam ... 245
Fruit crisps and dried fruit ... 246
Granola bars ... 252
Reduced sugar pecan praline ... 256
Soft nougat with aquafaba ... 258
Lactose-free soft caramels ... 260
Reduced sugar lollipops ... 262
Homemade chocolate bars with no white sugar ... 264
Gluten-free buckwheat and coffee bites ... 270
Sugar- and lactose-free coconut and cinnamon truffles ... 271

DECORATIONS AND ARTISTIC CENTREPIECES 272

Almond paste figures ... 274
Nougatine ... 278
Pastillage ... 280
Pressed sugar, poured sugar and royal icing ... 282
Pulled sugar ... 286
Valentine's Day centrepiece ... 290
Easter egg ... 294
Christmas tree ... 298
Artistic centrepiece ... 302

Glossary ... 306
Recipe index ... 309
Acknowledgements ... 310

THE ART OF CONFECTIONERY

Confectionery, whether sweets or chocolates, covers a wide repertoire of traditional and modern sweet confections. Steeped in history, confectionery is also part of a cultural and traditional heritage that contributes to the way of life in many countries, both in Europe and beyond.

Although the word "confectionery" first appeared in the 13th century, the art of making sweets dates back to before antiquity. The first sweets in the Middle East were made with honey, which was recognised for its excellent energising and therapeutic properties, and was appreciated for its flavour and the fact that it was easy to store. Fresh seasonal fruits were also used in confectionery, and techniques were developed to dry and preserve them, making them extra enjoyable. Both a gift from the gods and an indulgence, confectionery embodies a sense of luxury and divine sweetness.

In the Middle Ages, confectionery was limited to medicinal uses. Sold in the form of loaves or powdered – and exclusively by apothecaries for treating the sick – when cane sugar was introduced to Europe by the Crusaders, it cost the same as certain spices. This link between confectionery and medicine remained the norm for centuries. The first treatises about antidotes and books on agronomy attest to this and provide us with several recipes, including the predecessors of marzipan and nougat. Could medicine be behind some of the sweets we love so much today?

It was not until the 19th century and the surge in sugar beet production that confectionery became accessible to a wider public. Sugar began to be appreciated in cooking and went beyond being used simply for medicinal purposes, leading to the development of sugar confectionery around the world. In France, in particular, a variety of regional confectionery products emerged as a form of local identity; many of them are included in this book, such as ardoises from Angers and calissons from Provence, alongside international recipes such as marmalade, fudge and cremino.

Thanks to progressive innovation in sugar processing techniques, confectioners have been able to develop several families of products: cooked sugars (for boiled sweets such as berlingots and barley sugar); nougat and nougatine; caramel; gummy sweets and liquorice; fruit pastes and almond pastes; praline; dragées and pralines; fondants; pastilles and jelly confectionery. Confectioners have come up with myriad shapes, colours, textures and flavours!

Although often considered a separate profession, chocolate-making is also part of the confectionery family, and small moulded bonbons, truffles and many other sweets constitute "chocolate" confectionery products.

Today's technology allows professional confectioners to choose from a huge range of equipment for creating ever more complex, ingenious and delicious creations. Silicone mats, specific machines, biscuit cutters of all kinds, as well as chocolate dippers, candying trays, sugar lamps and increasingly high-performance thermometers, not to mention moulds, which are now made from a host of materials, including polycarbonate and silicone are all readily available. Some of these items are available in smaller formats for anyone wanting to learn or improve their skills at home.

Over the centuries, confectionery has evolved to remain at the height of the culinary arts and accessible to everyone. With changing fashions and a growing trend towards healthier products, new sweeteners – both natural and synthetic – have made their way into confectionery. With this in mind, Le Cordon Bleu has developed programmes covering both traditional and modern confectionery techniques, offering both professional training programmes and short courses for enthusiasts, with a focus on nutrition, health and plant-based ingredients.

Confectionery, a gourmet treat for yourself or as a gift, is also a delicate art form in which creations combine finesse, precision and beauty.

LE CORDON BLEU

LE CORDON BLEU
Key dates

1895   In Paris, French journalist Marthe Distel launches a culinary magazine called *La Cuisinière Cordon Bleu*. In October, the magazine's subscribers are invited to the first Le Cordon Bleu cooking classes.

1897   Le Cordon Bleu Paris welcomes its first Russian student.

1905   Le Cordon Bleu Paris trains its first Japanese student.

1914   Le Cordon Bleu now has four schools in Paris.

1927   On 16 November, the London *Daily Mail* reports on a visit to Le Cordon Bleu Paris: "It's not unusual to see eight different nationalities in a class."

1933   Rosemary Hume and Dione Lucas, trained at Le Cordon Bleu Paris under Chef Henri-Paul Pellaprat, open the Petit Cordon Bleu school and the Au Petit Cordon Bleu restaurant in London.

1942   Dione Lucas opens a Le Cordon Bleu school and restaurant in New York. She also writes the best-selling *The Cordon Bleu Cook Book* (1947) and becomes the first woman to host a TV cooking show in the United States.

1948   Le Cordon Bleu receives Pentagon accreditation for providing professional training to young American soldiers following their tour of service in Europe. Julia Child, a former member of the Office of Strategic Services (OSS) in the United States, begins her training at the Le Cordon Bleu Paris school.

1953   Le Cordon Bleu London creates the recipe for Coronation Chicken, which is served to foreign dignitaries at the coronation dinner of Her Majesty Queen Elizabeth II.

1954   The success of Billy Wilder's film *Sabrina*, starring Audrey Hepburn, contributes to Le Cordon Bleu's growing reputation.

1984   The Cointreau family, descendants of the founding families of the Rémy Martin and Cointreau liqueur brands, takes over the presidency of Le Cordon Bleu Paris from Elisabeth Brassart, who had been its director since 1945.

1988   Le Cordon Bleu Paris moves from rue du Champ de Mars, near the Eiffel Tower, to rue Léon Delhomme, in the 15th arrondissement; the school is inaugurated by the minister Édouard Balladur. • Le Cordon Bleu Ottawa welcomes its first students.

1991   Le Cordon Bleu Japan opens its doors in Tokyo, then in Kobe. The school is known as "Little France in Japan".

1995   Le Cordon Bleu celebrates its 100th anniversary. The Shanghai district authorities in China send chefs abroad for the first time to train at Le Cordon Bleu Paris.

1996 Le Cordon Bleu sets up in Sydney, Australia, at the request of the New South Wales government, training chefs in preparation for the Sydney 2000 Olympic Games. Bachelor's and Master's degrees in management, as well as university research in fields such as the hospitality industry, restaurants, culinary arts and wine are then introduced in Adelaide.

1998 Le Cordon Bleu signs an exclusive agreement with Career Education Corporation (CEC) to export its educational expertise to the United States, offering Associate Diplomas with unique content in culinary arts and hospitality management.

2002 Le Cordon Bleu Korea and Le Cordon Bleu Mexico open their doors to their first students.

2003 The adventure begins for Le Cordon Bleu Peru, where it has grown to become the leading culinary institute in the country.

2006 Le Cordon Bleu Thailand is launched in partnership with Dusit International.

2009 The entire Le Cordon Bleu network participates in the launch of the film *Julie & Julia*, starring Meryl Streep as Julia Child, a Le Cordon Bleu Paris alumna.

2011 Le Cordon Bleu Madrid opens in partnership with the Universidad Francisco de Vitoria. • Le Cordon Bleu launches its first online Master of Gastronomic Tourism programme.

2012 Le Cordon Bleu Malaysia is launched in partnership with Sunway University College. • Le Cordon Bleu London moves to Bloomsbury Square. • Le Cordon Bleu New Zealand opens in Wellington.

2013 Official opening of Le Cordon Bleu Istanbul. • Le Cordon Bleu Thailand receives the award for the Best Culinary School in Asia. • An agreement is signed with Ateneo de Manila University to open an institute in the Philippines.

2014 Le Cordon Bleu in India opens its doors and offers students university courses in hospitality and restaurant management. • Le Cordon Bleu Lebanon and Le Cordon Bleu Advanced Studies in Gastronomy (HEG) celebrate their 10th anniversary.

2015 The 120th anniversary of Le Cordon Bleu is celebrated around the world. • Le Cordon Bleu Shanghai welcomes its first students. • Le Cordon Bleu Taiwan opens its doors with NKUHT and the Ming-Tai Institute. • Le Cordon Bleu is inaugurated in Santiago de Chile in partnership with Finis Terrae University.

2016 Le Cordon Bleu Paris relocates to ultra-modern premises on the banks of the Seine in the 15th arrondissement, with 4,000m² dedicated to the culinary arts and wine, hospitality and restaurant management. • Le Cordon Bleu Paris also launches two Bachelor's degrees in partnership with the University of Paris Dauphine-PSL.

2018 Le Cordon Bleu Peru obtains university status.

2020 Le Cordon Bleu celebrates 125 years of teaching excellence. • Le Cordon Bleu opens the Signatures restaurant in Rio de Janeiro, Brazil, and launches certified online higher education programmes.

2021 Le Cordon Bleu's new programmes focus on innovation and health, with degrees dedicated to nutrition, well-being, vegetarian cuisine and food science. • Le Cordon Bleu offers a Master's Degree in *Culinary Innovation Management* in partnership with Birbeck, University of London.

2022 CORD by Le Cordon Bleu restaurant and café opens in London. • Le Cordon Bleu Paris is named Best Culinary Training Establishment in Europe and Best Culinary Training Establishment in the World at the World Culinary Awards. • In North America and Oceania, Le Cordon Bleu also receives the award for Best Culinary Training Establishment.

2023 Chosen by France's Ministry of Culture, Le Cordon Bleu Paris now provides culinary workshops and demonstrations, conferences and wine courses – at the iconic Hôtel de la Marine on place de la Concorde. • Le Cordon Bleu London offers a new *MSc Hospitality Innovation Management* in partnership with Birbeck, University of London.

LE CORDON BLEU
institutes throughout the world

LE CORDON BLEU PARIS
13–15, quai André Citroën
75015 Paris, France

Tel: +33 (0) 1 85 65 15 00
paris@cordonbleu.edu

LE CORDON BLEU LONDON
15 Bloomsbury Square
London WC1A 2LS
United Kingdom

Tel: +44 (0) 207 400 3900
london@cordonbleu.edu

LE CORDON BLEU MADRID
Universidad Francisco de Vitoria
Ctra. Pozuelo-Majadahonda
Km. 1,800
Pozuelo de Alarcón, 28223 Madrid,
Spain

Tel: +34 91 715 10 46
madrid@cordonbleu.edu

LE CORDON BLEU ISTANBUL
Özyeğin University
Çekmeköy Campus
Nişantepe Mevkii, Orman Sokak, No:13
Alemdağ, Çekmeköy 34794
Istanbul, Turkey

Tel: +90 216 564 9000
istanbul@cordonbleu.edu

LE CORDON BLEU LEBANON
Burj on Bay Hotel
Tabarja – Kfaryassine
Lebanon

Tel: +961 9 85 75 57
lebanon@cordonbleu.edu

LE CORDON BLEU JAPAN
Ritsumeikan University Biwako/
Kusatsu Campus
1 Chome-1-1 Nojihigashi
Kusatsu, Shiga 525–8577, Japan

Tel: +81 3 5489 0141
tokyo@cordonbleu.edu

LE CORDON BLEU KOREA
Sookmyung Women's University
7th Fl., Social Education Bldg.
Cheongpa-ro 47gil 100, Yongsan-Ku
Seoul, 140–742 Korea

Tel: +82 2 719 6961
korea@cordonbleu.edu

LE CORDON BLEU OTTAWA
453 Laurier Avenue East
Ottawa, Ontario, K1N 6R4, Canada

Tel: +1 613 236 CHEF (2433)
Toll free: +1 888 289 6302
Restaurant line: +1 613 236 2499
ottawa@cordonbleu.edu

LE CORDON BLEU MEXICO
Universidad Anáhuac North Campus
Universidad Anáhuac South Campus
Universidad Anáhuac Querétaro Campus
Universidad Anáhuac Cancún Campus
Universidad Anáhuac Mérida Campus
Universidad Anáhuac Puebla Campus
Universidad Anáhuac Tampico Campus
Universidad Anáhuac Oaxaca Campus
Av. Universidad Anáhuac No. 46, Col.
Lomas Anáhuac
Huixquilucan, Edo. De Mex. C.P. 52786,
Mexico City

Tel: +52 55 5627 0210 ext. 7132 / 7813
mexico@cordonbleu.edu

LE CORDON BLEU PERU
Universidad Le Cordon Bleu Peru
(ULCB)
Le Cordon Bleu Peru Instituto
Le Cordon Bleu Cordontec
Av. Vasco Núñez de Balboa 530
Miraflores, Lima 18, Peru

Tel: +51 1 617 8300
peru@cordonbleu.edu

LE CORDON BLEU AUSTRALIA
Le Cordon Bleu Adelaide Campus
Le Cordon Bleu Sydney Campus
Le Cordon Bleu Melbourne Campus
Le Cordon Bleu Brisbane Campus
Days Road, Regency Park
South Australia 5010, Australia

Free call (Australia only):
1 800 064 802
Tel: +61 8 8346 3000
australia@cordonbleu.edu

LE CORDON BLEU NEW ZEALAND
52 Cuba Street
Wellington, 6011, New Zealand

Tel: +64 4 4729800
nz@cordonbleu.edu

LE CORDON BLEU MALAYSIA
Sunway University
No. 5, Jalan Universiti, Bandar Sunway
46150 Petaling Jaya, Selangor DE,
Malaysia

Tel: +603 5632 1188
malaysia@cordonbleu.edu

LE CORDON BLEU THAILAND

4, 4/5 Zen tower, 17th-19th floor
Central World
Ratchadamri Road, Pathumwan
Subdistrict, 10330
Pathumwan District, Bangkok 10330
Thailand

Tel: +66 2 237 8877
thailand@cordonbleu.edu

LE CORDON BLEU SHANGHAI

2F, Building 1, No 1458 Pu Dong
Nan Road
Shanghai, China 200122

Tel: +86 400 118 1895
shanghai@cordonbleu.edu

LE CORDON BLEU INDIA

G D Goenka University
Sohna Gurgaon Road
Sohna, Haryana
India

Tel: +91 880 099 20 22 / 23 / 24
lcb@gdgoenka.ac.in

LE CORDON BLEU CHILE

Universidad Finis Terrae
Avenida Pedro de Valdivia 1509
Providencia
Santiago de Chile, Chile

Tel: +56 24 20 72 23

LE CORDON BLEU RIO DE JANEIRO

Rua da Passagem, 179, Botafogo
Rio de Janeiro, RJ, 22290-031
Brazil

Tel: +55 21 9940-02117
riodejaneiro@cordonbleu.edu

LE CORDON BLEU SÃO PAULO

Rua Natingui, 862 Primero andar
Vila Madalena, SP, São Paulo
05443-001
Brazil

Tel: +55 11 3185-2500
saopaulo@cordonbleu.edu

LE CORDON BLEU TAIWAN

National Kaohsiung University
of Hospitality and Tourism
No 1, Songhe Rd
Xiaogang Dist., Kaohsiung City
81271 Taiwan Region

Tel: +886 (07) 801 0909 /
0800-307688
taiwan@cordonbleu.edu

LE CORDON BLEU MANILA

G/F George SK Ty Learning
Innovation Wing, Areté, Ateneo
de Manila University, Katipunan
Avenue 1108
Quezon City, Philippines

Tel: +632 8426.6001 loc. 5381 and
5384

www.cordonbleu.edu
e-mail: info@cordonbleu.edu

Confectionery techniques

THE INGREDIENTS
used in confectionery

SUGARS

Sugar and sweeteners are essential ingredients in confectionery. Whether it comes from sugar cane or sugar beet, sugar is practically pure sucrose. There are many types of sugar on the market.

UNREFINED RAW SUGAR
Unrefined cane sugar from the first stage of sugar crystallisation.

MOLASSES
A thick syrup produced by refining cane sugar or sugar beet.

WHITE GRANULATED SUGAR
Sugar obtained by crystallising sugar syrups from sugar mills or refineries, resulting in sugar with crystals of differing fineness.

SUGAR CUBES
Moistened granulated sugar is heated and moulded; it is then dried, which makes the granules stick together. As this kind of sugar contains very few impurities (e.g. dust), it is considered very pure and is often used when creating artistic sugar work.

CASTER SUGAR
The most widely consumed sugar, it is made from sugar cane or sugar beet, and usually comes in the form of a fine white powder.

ICING SUGAR
Made by grinding white granulated sugar – which may or not be refined – to a very fine powder. It is then sifted and 3% of its weight in starch is added to prevent clumping. This type of sugar dissolves very quickly.

MUSCOVADO SUGAR
Unrefined cane sugar with a high molasses content and a distinctive taste.

SOFT BROWN SUGAR
Refined beet or cane sugar that is coloured (light or dark brown) and has a soft consistency. Light and dark brown vergeoise sugar is available in shops.

NATURAL SUGARS

HONEY
Used to add softness, texture and sweetness to recipes (e.g. nougat). Whether mono-floral or multi-floral, honeys have different organoleptic qualities. These range from very mild, with an almost odourless taste, to very pronounced, and can vary from very pale yellow to dark brown.

MAPLE SYRUP
Obtained from the sap of the maple tree.

BIRCH OR XYLITOL SUGAR
A sugar alcohol (polyol) found in birch bark.

COCONUT SUGAR
An unrefined sugar made from the sap of *Cocos nucifera* flowers.

The ingredients used in confectionery

OTHER SWEETENING AGENTS

GLUCOSE
Most often in the form of a colourless syrup with a thick, viscous texture, it is also available in powdered form (atomised). Derived from maize starch or potato starch, glucose is an anti-crystallising agent and preservative.

ISOMALT
A sugar alcohol (polyol) produced by transforming sucrose into a combination of glucose, sorbitol and mannitol using enzymes and hydrogenation. It is sold in the form of opaque white granules, very similar to sugar.

MALTITOL
A disaccharide polyol derived from maize or barley, it is used as a sugar substitute and stabiliser. It is made by hydrogenating maltose.

TREHALOSE
A disaccharide obtained from tapioca starch.

TRIMOLINE® (INVERTED SUGAR)
A mixture of fructose and glucose obtained from cane sugar or sucrose by acid hydrolysis. Valued for its anti-drying properties, it stops sugar from crystallising and enhances flavour. For quantities of less than 15 g, honey can be used as a substitute.

CHOCOLATE

A number of cocoa products, which come from the beans of the cocoa tree, are used in confectionery. The three main varieties of cocoa, which thrive in tropical lands, are *criollo* (a low yield but highly sought-after quality), *forastero* (a high yield but with a less distinctive taste) and *trinitario* (a hybrid of *criollo* and *forastero*).

COCOA BUTTER
A fat with an almost neutral taste and a faint aroma of cocoa, which is released after cocoa beans have been ground during the cocoa powder manufacturing process. It is an ingredient in chocolate making.

UNSWEETENED COCOA POWDER
Obtained after the cocoa mass is pressed and a quantity of cocoa butter has been separated. The remaining mass is ground into a fine powder containing about 20% cocoa butter.

COUVERTURE CHOCOLATE
High-quality chocolate containing a minimum of 31% cocoa butter. Because of its specific properties, this kind of chocolate is used for tempering.

COCOA BEANS
The cocoa seeds contained in a cacao pod, which is the fruit of the cacao tree.

MYCRYO®
Cocoa butter that has been cryogenically frozen and comes in powdered form. When a small amount is added, it makes tempering chocolate easier and makes couverture chocolate glossy and with a good snap.

COCOA MASS
A paste obtained by grinding cocoa beans. It is the raw material for all cocoa- and chocolate-based products.

OTHER INGREDIENTS

ACIDIFYING AGENT
A product that helps accelerate gelling, enhance flavours and preserve the colour of fruit-based preparations. It acts as an anti-crystallising agent during the cooking of sugar syrups and aids the ability of sugars to absorb moisture, making cooked sugars more malleable. The main acidifying agents used in confectionery are citric acid, tartaric acid and cream of tartar.

AQUAFABA
The protein-rich liquid obtained when cooking pulses (usually chickpeas). It can be used as a replacement for egg whites as a foaming agent. It can also be used as a thickener and emulsifier. Aquafaba contains plant proteins that are easier to digest and, above all, less allergenic than the proteins in egg whites. To make your own aquafaba, soak 250 g of chickpeas in 1 kg of water overnight. The next day, drain and cover with water, then cook until tender but still slightly firm. Drain the chickpeas, keeping the aquafaba (cooking water) and leave to cool.

FLAVOURING
An ingredient that imparts or enhances a flavour (smell or taste). These can be natural flavourings (either animal or plant based) or flavourings that are identical to natural ones (synthetic but chemically identical to natural flavourings).

FOOD COLOURING
A natural or synthetic food additive used to enhance or give colour to confectionery. It comes in various forms: liquid, gel or powder. It is important to distinguish between water-soluble food colouring, to be mixed with water or alcohol (recommended for colouring foods such as almond paste, etc.) and fat-soluble ones (used for chocolate, butters, etc.).

SPIRITS – BRANDY (EAU-DE-VIE)
Alcoholic beverages obtained by distilling wine, the fermented juice of certain fruits or food substances (e.g. kirsch, made from cherries).

CORNFLOUR
A very fine white powder extracted from maize starch, it is finer than maize flour.

POTATO STARCH
A fine white powder obtained from dried potatoes ground into flour.

WAFER SHEET
Made from unleavened wafer dough, is also known as nougat wafer or communion bread. In confectionery, it is used to wrap nougat and as a base for calissons and other specialities so that you can enjoy them without your fingers getting sticky.

GELATINE
Whether powdered or in transparent sheet form, gelatine is a substance extracted from the collagen found in the skin and bones of cattle, pigs and fish. There is little difference between powdered and sheet gelatine. It sets at a temperature of between 24°C and 26°C and is fully set after 16 hours.

EVAPORATED MILK (UNSWEETENED)
Vacuum-packed concentrated whole milk, from which 60% of the water has been removed, it is then sterilised and packaged. The result is a thick milk that is creamy in colour.

SWEETENED CONDENSED MILK
Unlike evaporated milk, a large amount of sugar is added to the milk, which is then concentrated in a vacuum before being cooled and packaged.

MARGARINE
An emulsion made of vegetable oil and water, similar in appearance to butter.

ALMOND PASTE
A confectionery preparation made from skinned almonds and hot or cold sugar, added in varying proportions.

PECTIN
A plant-based product used for its stabilising, gelling and thickening properties. The most common pectins are NH pectin and yellow pectin.

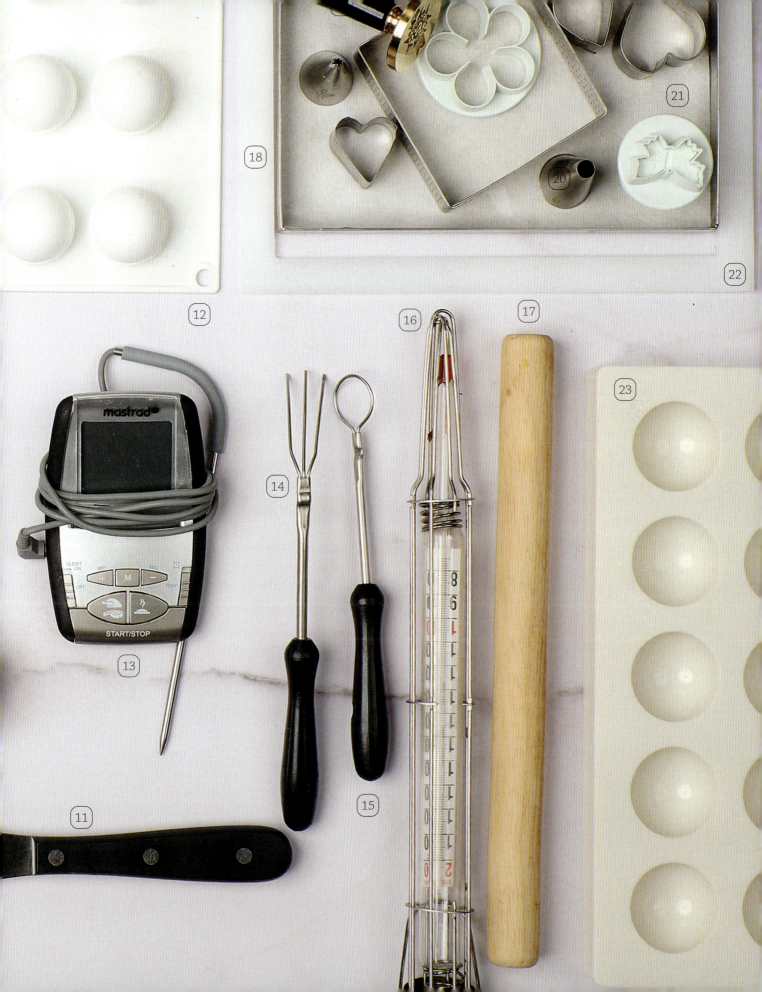

Confectionery equipment

PASTRY FRAME AND RING (18)(22)
Stainless steel or silicone frames and rings of various diameters (from 6 to 34 cm) and heights, used in confectionery (poured sugar, caramel). They are also available with a base (stainless steel tray).

CANDISSOIRE (1)
Also known as a candissoire tray. Usually rectangular, it is a stainless steel tray with high sides and a 9 × 9 mm rack on which to place, drain, rest and dry ingredients being candied.

CHEF'S BLOWTORCH
A gas blowtorch used for flambéing and caramelising. It is also used to heat stainless steel bowls to keep a preparation warm (e.g. nougat).

CHINA CAP SIEVE (CHINOIS)
A conical metal strainer used to filter thick preparations. Some china cap sieves have a very fine mesh, and these are used for filtering more liquid preparations.

STARCH TRAY (SEE P. 43)
A wooden-sided tray filled with a mixture of wheat starch and cornflour in equal quantities. Imprints are made at regular intervals in the starch, then filled with jelly sweets, liqueur fillings etc.

PLASTIC DOUGH SCRAPER
A flat, half-moon-shaped utensil for scraping containers used in cuisine or pastry.

PARING KNIFE (8)
A small knife with a short, pointed blade used for trimming, peeling and cutting small things.

BAKER'S SERRATED KNIFE (7)
A flexible, robust knife with a stainless steel blade (serrated blade with a rounded tip) for cutting delicate foods without damaging them.

COPPER
Copper pots and saucepans are recommended when making confectionery because of their heat-conducting properties.

PASTRY CUTTER -> BISCUIT CUTTER

DEHYDRATOR
An electric appliance with fine mesh racks for drying slices of food, in which heated air circulates for several hours.

PIPING NOZZLE (19)(20)
Hollow, conical nozzles made of stainless steel or polycarbonate, inserted into a piping bag to pipe preparations onto a baking tray or used for decorating. Nozzles can be plain, fluted or a special shape (Saint-Honoré, petal, basket-weave, etc.).

SKIMMER
A large, flat, metal mesh spoon with a long handle, used to skim foam from the surface of preparations. It can also be used to take ingredients out of the liquid in which they have been blanched.

BISCUIT CUTTER (21)
Also known as a pastry cutter. A metal or plastic utensil available in a variety of shapes (round, oval, semi-circular, etc.), which is pressed into the dough to cut out neat shapes.

PISTON FUNNEL
A conical metal utensil with a nozzle that closes hermetically, it is used to pour small quantities of liquid or foamy preparations into moulds or containers. Alternatively you can use a jug or a spoon.

SOFT ACETATE GUITAR SHEETS
Thin sheets of transparent polyethylene suitable for contact with food, they are used in many ways in pastry and chocolate making. They can be used as a work surface for sugar decorations, to add glossiness to chocolate, for leaving just-coated bonbons to harden, or for spreading sugar paste.

WHISK (9)
A utensil that makes mixing or emulsifying preparations or batters/creams easy.

DIPPING FORK (CHOCOLATE) (14)(15)

With a ring (round) or with tines (2, 3 or 4 tines) on a shaft attached to a handle, it is slipped under the item to be dipped, then gently submerged into tempered chocolate. It can also be used to make decorations.

SUGAR LAMP

Used to heat cooked sugar so that it stays supple and malleable and can be worked into ribbons, decorations, etc. The lamp is usually placed on a stainless steel work surface and is fitted with a very resistant ceramic lamp that is attached to a flex so that the height and heat can be adjusted as necessary.

SILICONE OR POLYCARBONATE MOULD (FOR CHOCOLATE) (12)(23)

Myriad shapes are available today. Silicone ones are extremely flexible, allowing very detailed creations to be made. Polycarbonate ones are very rigid, giving chocolate a highly glossy sheen.

PASTRY BRUSH (3)

A tool with fibres or bristles attached to a handle and used for soaking or gently cleaning (e.g. starch from the surface of a food). In chocolate making, a pastry brush is useful for brushing liquid or powdered food colouring into moulds.

REFRACTOMETER (10)

A high-precision optical device that determines degrees Brix and is used to measure the diluted sugar content in a solution. It is essential for achieving consistent preparations.

RULER (5)

A tool marked in centimetres or inches for drawing straight lines and measuring lengths for precise cutting.

METAL CONFECTIONERY RULER (4)

Metal rods, often sold in pairs, used to achieve a uniform thickness of a preparation rolled out on a flat surface. Several heights are available, including the most common that measure 1 cm to 1.5 cm.

RHODOÏD® (ACETATE)

Sheets or strips of quite thick, rigid plastic used to line dessert rings and for chocolate making. Their smooth, shiny surface means they are easy to remove from a mould, and they make chocolate decorations glossy. Tempered chocolate spread with a spatula or knife onto a PVC sheet, then cut into a shape and left to harden results in a glossy surface.

ROLLING PINS (17)

Cylindrical in shape and traditionally made of wood, they are used to flatten dough. They come in different sizes and thicknesses depending on what they are needed for. Heavy stainless steel rollers are available for nougatine and cooked sugar.

METAL SPATULAS AND WIDE STAINLESS STEEL SPATULAS (11)

Multi-purpose utensils, straight or offset, long or short, they are used mainly for spreading and smoothing preparations such as ganache or icing. To temper chocolate, we recommend using a wide stainless steel spatula.

SILICONE SPATULAS (2)

These have a rounded silicone blade attached to a long handle. They are used to gently mix delicate mixtures or to scrape all the mixture from the bottom of bowls so that it can be transferred more easily to a piping bag or mould.

SIEVE AND DRUM SIEVE

A rounded stainless steel utensil with a stainless steel mesh, used to ensure that dry ingredients or mixtures are uniform in texture. Cooked food can be pressed through it to make a purée.

SILICONE MAT (6)

A silicone-impregnated material embedded with woven glass-fibres, usually the size of a baking tray. They are heat resistant, non-stick and can be used instead of baking parchment. Ideal when baking confectionery on a tray, as well as for working with sugar and nougatine. Another mat, Silpain®, is a perforated mat that allows moisture and steam to escape during baking, resulting in crispy baked goods.

COOKING THERMOMETER (10)(13)(16)

A utensil often fitted with a probe to measure the precise temperature of a food or preparation during cooking. Laser models can be used to read the temperature of chocolate or the surface of a food, but cannot be used to measure the temperature of cooked sugar syrup or foods which let off steam. A sugar thermometer is a glass tube with a scale containing a liquid that expands to give the temperature.

Cooking sugar

FOR 2.35 LITRES OF SYRUP AT 30° BAUMÉ

DIFFICULTY
Preparation time: 5 min • **Cooking time:** 5 min

INGREDIENTS
1 litre water • 1.35 kg sugar

EQUIPMENT
1 copper saucepan • 1 pastry brush • 1 cooking thermometer

- Pour the water and sugar into a clean, dry saucepan. Stir to dissolve the sugar, then bring to the boil (up to the moment it boils, make sure you keep the sides of the saucepan clean with the brush dipped in water. There may be dust or other impurities in the sugar which, when heated, will form a foam on the surface of the syrup).

- Skim off any impurities with a skimmer or a tablespoon just as it comes to the boil.

CHEF'S TIPS

Copper is recommended for its heat-conducting properties. If you don't have a copper saucepan, use a heavy-bottomed stainless steel one. • If the sugar is heated to a temperature higher than what you desire, it can be cooled by adding a little water to the saucepan. Simply continue cooking until the desired temperature is reached. However, once it reaches 170°C, you cannot add water to cooked sugar. • The quality of the sugar is also important: sugar cubes are drier, often purer and less dusty. They are used mainly to make decorative sugar elements and for pulled sugar.

TIPS FOR COOKING SUGAR

- Sugar is a water-soluble substance, so not much water is needed to dissolve it: 180 g of sugar can be dissolved in about 100 g of water at room temperature. This is called the saturation point. However, the higher the temperature of the water, the more soluble the sugar becomes.

- Make sure the sugar has dissolved completely in the water before you start cooking it: place the water in a saucepan, add the sugar and wait for it to dissolve entirely before heating the saucepan.

- Sugar should be cooked gradually, and at each stage of cooking there is a physical change corresponding to density. The higher the temperature of the syrup, the more water evaporates and the denser and harder the syrup will become when cooled.

- Be careful not to stir the sugar syrup once it has come to the boil as it may crystallise.

- The stages of the sugar can be tested either using a thermometer (a probe or sugar thermometer) or by hand. Before the advent of thermometers, professionals simply measured sugar syrups by hand as they cooked. This method is very useful, in particular for small quantities of syrup. But be careful, once the hard crack stage has been reached and the sugar has started to colour, this way of testing can be dangerous.

- To test by hand – without burning yourself – prepare a bowl of iced water. Dip your fingertips and thumb in the water to cool them, then quickly scoop a little sugar syrup from the saucepan and put it into the iced water to test its consistency (you can also use a teaspoon to do this).

- If using a cooking thermometer, make sure it is accurately calibrated and correctly positioned in the saucepan. The tip of the probe must be in the centre of the saucepan and must not touch the bottom or the reading will be inaccurate. The temperature indicated by a thermometer for small quantities is not always accurate.

SUGAR COOKING STAGES

- At 100°C, sugar syrup comes to the boil. The quantities in the recipe opposite correspond to a 30° Baumé syrup. The syrup is now liquid and can be used for imbibing. Flavouring or food colouring can now be added.

- At 104°C and above, the sugar will be thicker. If you take a drop between your thumb and forefinger, you will see a small, very fine thread form as you separate your fingers.

- At 110°C, this thread is longer and stronger.

- Between 117°C and 119°C, the syrup is at soft ball stage. If you take a spoonful of this syrup and immerse it in a bowl of cold water, it will form a soft ball. Sugar at this stage is often used in pastries and confectionery.

- Between 120°C and 124°C, the syrup is at firm ball stage. This is now ideal for making Italian meringues, fondants, caramel, etc. Submerging the sugar in cold water produces a much firmer ball.

- At 125°C and above, the syrup is cooked to hard ball stage, which is even firmer.

- At 130°C and above, the syrup is cooked to soft crack stage. At this stage, the syrup is denser and hardens immediately if poured into cold water. It is brittle, but will stick to your teeth.

- At 145°C, the syrup is cooked to hard crack stage. When poured into cold water, a drop of syrup becomes as brittle as glass and no longer sticks to your teeth.

- At 150°C and above, the sugar begins to change colour. The moisture in the syrup has evaporated and the remaining sugar starts to darken. At first it is golden, becoming barley-coloured at about 155°C, then light caramel, blond, amber, darkening all the way to brown. At this stage, the temperature rises very quickly and the colour gets darker and darker.

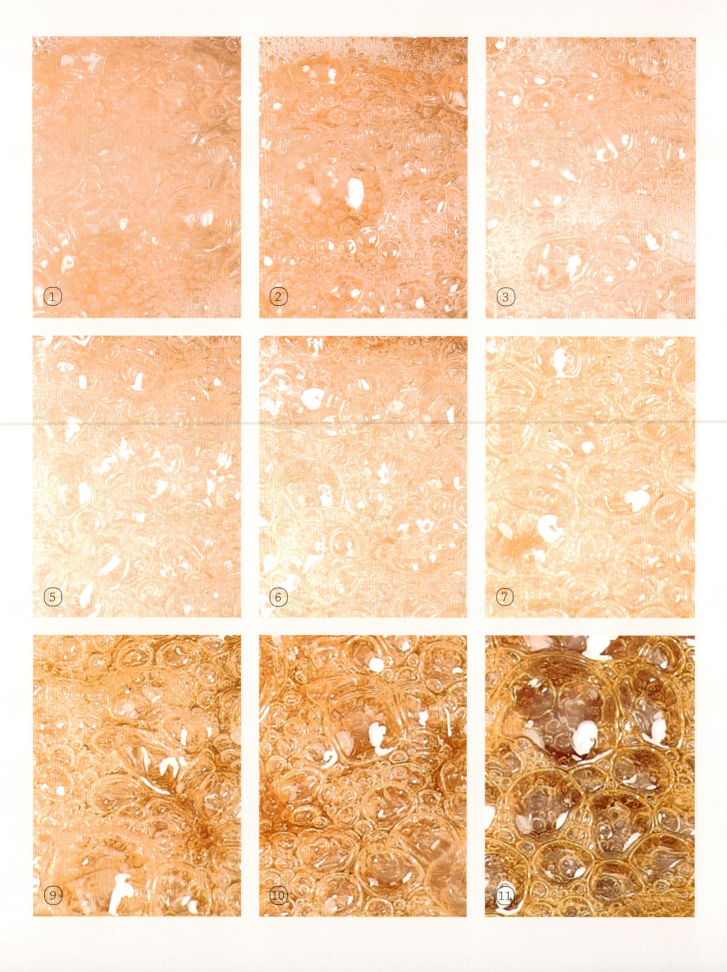

The temperature chart (below) lists the various stages of sugar cooking. The changes are gradual with the evaporation of water. The names are an indication but it is preferable to rely on the readings of the thermometer.

SUGAR TEMPERATURE CHART

	SUGAR STAGE	TEMPERATURE
	Boiling	100°C
	Long thread	103°C
1	Small pearl	104°C
2	Short thread	105-106°C
	Large pearl	107°C
3	Thread	110°C
	Soufflé	113-114°C
	Feather	115-116°C
4	Soft ball	117-119°C
5	Firm ball	120-124°C
6	Hard ball	125-128°C
7	Soft crack	130-140°C
8	Hard crack	145-149°C
9	Sugar light yellow	150°C
10	Barley-coloured sugar	155-160°C
11	Caramel	161-180°C

THE DIFFERENT COLOURS OF SUGAR AS IT REACTS TO PROGRESSIVELY HIGHER HEAT

Candying
Candied orange peel

FOR 20 CANDIED ORANGE PEEL QUARTERS

DIFFICULTY ○○○

Preparation time: 8 days • Freezing time: 1 h • Cooking time: 40 min

INGREDIENTS

5 untreated oranges • 2 litres water • ½ tsp bicarbonate of soda • glucose for the 8th day

SYRUP

1.5 litres water • 600 g sugar • 425 g glucose

EQUIPMENT

1 refractometer

DAY 1

- Wash the oranges, place in a saucepan with plenty of water and bring to the boil for 10 minutes (1). Using a skimmer, lift the oranges from the saucepan and place in a large bowl of iced water to cool (2).

- Drain the oranges, then use a paring knife to make a cross-shaped incision in the peel to create equal quarters. Remove the skin, taking care not to lift off the pith (3). Place the peels in a container in the freezer until frozen (about 1 hour).

- Put the frozen peels in a saucepan with the 2 kg of cold water and the bicarbonate of soda. Bring gently to the boil over a medium heat, then remove the peels as they rise to the surface. Rinse under cold water and set aside.

SYRUP

- Pour the water and sugar into a large saucepan, stir to dissolve the sugar, then add the glucose and bring to the boil.

- Place the peels in a large bowl and pour the syrup over them. Cover with baking parchment in direct contact with them and leave at room temperature overnight (4).

DAY 2

- Pour the syrup from the peels into a saucepan, leaving the peels in the bowl.

- Boil the syrup for about 2 minutes until the refractometer reaches 50° Brix (see p. 31 and 306). Pour the syrup over the peels. Cover with baking parchment in direct contact with them and leave at room temperature overnight.

DAY 3

- Pour the syrup from the peels into a saucepan, leaving the peels in the bowl. Bring the syrup to the boil for about 2 minutes, until the density reaches 52° Brix on the refractometer. Pour the syrup over the peels, making sure they are all well covered.
- Leave at room temperature overnight, covered with baking parchment in direct contact with them.

DAY 4

- Repeat the same operation as the previous days, bringing the syrup to a density of 55° Brix.

DAY 5

- Repeat the same operation as the previous days, bringing the syrup to a density of 57° Brix.

DAY 6

- Repeat the same operation as the previous days, bringing the syrup to a density of 60° Brix.

DAY 7

- Repeat the same operation as the previous days, bringing the syrup to a density of 63° Brix.

DAY 8

- Using a clean spoon, remove the peels from the syrup and set aside in another bowl. Weigh the syrup and add 10% of its weight in glucose. Bring the syrup to the boil for about 2 minutes to reach a density of 66° Brix (be careful not to go higher than 70° Brix or the syrup may recrystallise). Pour the syrup over the peels, making sure they are all well covered. Cover with baking parchment in direct contact with them.
- When cool, store the peels with the syrup in an airtight container until ready to use. If the peel is properly candied, it will keep for at least a year.

CHEF'S TIPS

Make sure that all the equipment used in the recipe is clean. • Throughout the process, make sure you have enough syrup to cover the peels, topping up with extra syrup if necessary. • Choose a saucepan big enough so that the peels are fully submerged. • Other types of citrus fruit can be prepared in the same way. For other kinds of fruit, the time needed to candy them may vary depending on the texture of the fruit.

Strawberry flavoured syrup

FOR 450 ML OF FLAVOURED SYRUP

DIFFICULTY ◯
Preparation time: 30 min • **Resting time:** 27 h • **Cooking time:** 35 min

INGREDIENTS
1.2 kg fresh strawberries • 1.2 kg sugar • 1 vanilla pod

EQUIPMENT
1 china cap sieve • 1 muslin cloth • 1 cooking thermometer
• 2 sterilised 225 ml jam jars

- Wash and dry the strawberries, then place them in a large bowl. Add the sugar and mix (1). Cover the bowl with cling film and leave to macerate for 3 hours at room temperature.

- Split and scrape the seeds from the vanilla pod with the tip of a knife. Pour the macerated mixture into a large saucepan and bring to the boil over a high heat. Boil for 5 minutes, then remove from the heat and add the vanilla seeds. Leave the syrup to cool at room temperature. When cool, cover with cling film and leave to stand for 24 hours at room temperature.

- The next day, strain the syrup through a china cap sieve lined with muslin set over a saucepan (2). Do not press it as this will make the syrup cloudy.

- Heat over medium heat and reduce the syrup for about 30 minutes, until the temperature reaches 105°C (3) (short thread, see p. 33), then skim off any foam from the surface. Strain the syrup into the 2 sterilised jars. Close and store in a dark place for up to 3 months.

CHEF'S TIPS

The pulp from pressed strawberries can be reused and blended using a hand-held blender; some of it can then be used in a fruit jelly recipe.
• Fresh raspberries can also be used instead of strawberries.

Candy syrup

Candy syrup is used as a finish for sweets such as ravioli (see p. 66).

FOR 3.5 LITRES OF CANDY SYRUP

DIFFICULTY

Preparation time: 10 min • **Resting time:** 30 min • **Cooking time:** 10 min

INGREDIENTS
1 litre water • 2.5 kg sugar

- Pour the water and sugar into a large saucepan and stir until the sugar has dissolved. Bring slowly to the boil over medium heat and skim off any impurities (foam that forms on the surface of the syrup) with a tablespoon or skimmer.
- Remove the saucepan from the heat, leave to cool, then cover with baking parchment in direct contact with the syrup. Leave to cool at room temperature without moving the saucepan.

USING CANDY SYRUP

- When candy syrup is used as a finish, the product (bonbons, almond paste figures, etc.) is placed in a candissoire tray and sometimes brushed with a thin layer of cocoa butter; the syrup is then poured in slowly, until it covers it completely.
- A rack is placed on top, along with a cloth or baking parchment to keep the product submerged. The tray should be left to stand for about 12 to 24 hours, to allow the sugar in the syrup to crystallise around the product (it should not be left for more than 24 hours if it is to be eaten).
- The product is then drained and placed on the rack of a candissoire tray to dry, either at room temperature or in a warming oven. As it dries, the surface of the product will become covered with small, shiny crystals.

Fondant

Fondant is a smooth, white, opaque paste made from sugar syrup cooked with glucose, then cooled and worked by incorporating air into it. A basic element of confectionery, it can also be coloured or flavoured with the main flavour of your creations.

FOR 350 G OF FONDANT

DIFFICULTY
Preparation time: 1 h • **Refrigeration time:** 3 days before use
Cooking time: 15 min

INGREDIENTS
90 ml water • 300 g sugar • 30 g glucose

EQUIPMENT
1 cooking thermometer • 1 stand mixer • 1 silicone mat

- Prepare a bowl of cold water larger than the saucepan.
- Pour the water and sugar into a saucepan and stir until the sugar has dissolved. Bring to the boil, then add the glucose. Heat until the temperature reaches 116°C (feather) on the cooking thermometer.
- Dip the bottom of the hot saucepan in the cold water to stop the syrup cooking. Carefully pour the hot syrup into the bowl of the mixer fitted with a paddle attachment. Beat at medium speed until the syrup is white, thickens and becomes opaque (1). Pour onto the silicone mat that has been moistened with cold water.
- Spread the fondant by pushing it in front of you with the palm of your hand several times (2) until it is uniform, smooth and supple (3).
- Leave the fondant to stand for at least 3 days at room temperature in an airtight container before using. Fondant will keep for up to 1 year in an airtight container.

CHEF'S TIPS

Contact with the air will cause the fondant to crust. To avoid this, wrap it well in baking parchment. • Glucose is added to prevent the sugar from crystallising. • Fondant can be reheated for a few seconds in the microwave to soften it if necessary.

Almond paste

Almond paste is a mixture of blanched almonds combined with sugar syrup. The flavour depends on the type and percentage of almonds used, which can vary between 20% and 60% of the total weight of the paste. A versatile ingredient, it lends itself to numerous recipes, such as calissons (see p. 144).

FOR 600 G OF ALMOND PASTE

DIFFICULTY
Preparation time: 1 h • Cooking time: 20 min

INGREDIENT
150 g whole almonds

COOKED SUGAR SYRUP
120 ml water • 300 g sugar • 60 g glucose

EQUIPMENT
1 food processor • 1 cooking thermometer

- Bring a large quantity of water to the boil in a saucepan, then leave the almonds in it for 5 minutes. Using a skimmer, remove the almonds and place them in a bowl of iced water. Skin the almonds (1), then dry the blanched almonds on kitchen paper.

- Place the blanched almonds in the bowl of a food processor and grind to a fine powder.

COOKED SUGAR SYRUP

- Pour the water and sugar into a saucepan, stir until the sugar dissolves, then add the glucose. Heat to 120°C (firm ball), checking with the thermometer.

- Carefully drizzle the hot syrup over the almonds in the food processor (2), then pulse several times until a paste begins to form (3). Continue to grind until the paste is smooth in texture, but do not let it heat too much.

- Take the paste out of the food processor and roll until smooth (4).

- Almond paste will keep for up to 3 weeks in an airtight container at room temperature, or wrapped in cling film.

Starch tray

FOR 1 30 X 50 CM STARCH TRAY

DIFFICULTY ♙♙

Preparation time: 30 min • Resting time: 4 days

INGREDIENTS
1.5 kg wheat starch • 1.5 kg cornflour

EQUIPMENT
1 wooden tray measuring 30 x 50 cm x 5 cm high, or 1 tray with high sides • 1 drum sieve • Stamps in a range of shapes and sizes

- Preheat the oven to 60°C. Mix the wheat starch and cornflour, then spread it evenly in the wooden tray.

- Dry the starch mixture out in the oven for 4 days, turning it over several times with a whisk (1) during the drying time to aerate it; this allows the moisture to evaporate evenly. This step is important to ensure that the starch mixture is perfectly dry.

- Remove the starch mixture from the oven, cool and then sieve (2). Fill the wooden tray again to the top with the mixture and pack it down well.

- Set aside the excess starch for sieving over the moulds once they have been filled.

- Smooth the top with a ruler to obtain a flat surface (3).

- Press imprints of the shape and size of your choice at regular intervals into the starch mixture, leaving a space of at least 1 cm between each one (some professionals glue plaster imprints at regular intervals onto a wooden ruler) (4).

CHEF'S TIP

Keep the tray in a stable, flat place.

Praline paste

FOR 230 G OF PRALINE PASTE

DIFFICULTY ♟

Preparation time: 10 min • **Cooking time:** 15 min

INGREDIENTS

75 g blanched almonds • 75 g blanched hazelnuts
• 30 ml water • 150 g sugar

Grapeseed oil for the baking tray

EQUIPMENT

1 food processor

- Preheat the oven to 170°C. Place the almonds and hazelnuts on a baking tray and bake for 10 minutes. Keep the nuts warm.

- Bring the water and sugar to the boil in a saucepan. Add the almonds and hazelnuts and stir with a wooden spatula. Remove from the heat and continue to stir until the almonds and hazelnuts turn white. Return to the heat and melt the sugar that has crystallised (1).

- When the nuts are caramelised and start making a sound, spread them out on an oiled baking tray (2). Leave to cool.

- Break the praline into pieces. Grind them in the food processor to a fine powder, then to a soft paste (3): to achieve this, stop the mixer frequently and stir with a silicone spatula.

Tempering
chocolate over a bain-marie

Adjust the amount of dark chocolate used according to the recipe of your choice.

FOR 300 G OF TEMPERED CHOCOLATE

DIFFICULTY
Preparation time: 15 min

INGREDIENTS
300 g dark couverture chocolate 70%

EQUIPMENT
1 cooking thermometer

- Chop the dark chocolate and prepare a large bowl filled with iced water. Melt the chocolate over a bain-marie: the water should simmer, but not boil, and never come into contact with the chocolate in the bowl, otherwise the chocolate will become dull and lose its fluidity (1). The temperature of the chocolate should reach 45°C on the cooking thermometer.

- When the temperature reaches 45 °C, remove the bowl of chocolate from the bain-marie and place it in the bowl of cold water, stirring continuously with a stiff spatula to cool the chocolate to 27°C (2).

- Remove the bowl of chocolate from the bowl of cold water. Reheat it over the bain-marie, stirring gently, in several steps, to ensure the bowl does not overheat and rapidly raise the temperature of the chocolate. When the chocolate reaches a temperature of 32°C (maximum) (3), remove immediately from the bain-marie. It should be smooth and shiny.

- Test the chocolate to ensure it is well tempered and ready to use. (See p. 50.)

CHEF'S TIPS

For milk chocolate, the chocolate is melted at 45°C, cooled to 26°C, then reheated to 29°C. • For white chocolate, it is melted at 40°C, cooled to 25°C, then reheated to 28°C. • Refer to the instructions provided by the brand of chocolate used, as temperatures may vary.

Tempering
chocolate by seeding

Adjust the amount of dark chocolate used according to the recipe of your choice.

FOR 300 G OF TEMPERED CHOCOLATE

DIFFICULTY

Preparation time: 20 min

INGREDIENTS

300 g dark couverture chocolate 70%

EQUIPMENT

1 cooking thermometer

- Heat two-thirds of the dark chocolate to 45 to 50°C on the cooking thermometer. (1).
- Remove from the bain-marie and add the remaining third of chocolate. (2). Stir until the added chocolate has melted and cooled the mass to between 30 and 32°C (3).
- Test the chocolate to ensure it is well tempered and ready to use. (See p. 50.)

CHEF'S TIP

If you are using bars of chocolate, chop before tempering to ensure even melting.

Tempering chocolate with Mycryo®

Adjust the amount of dark chocolate used according to the recipe of your choice.

FOR 300 G OF TEMPERED CHOCOLATE

DIFFICULTY
Preparation time: 15 min

INGREDIENTS
300 g dark couverture chocolate 70%
• 3 g Mycryo® cocoa butter (1 % of the chocolate mass)

EQUIPMENT
1 cooking thermometer • 1 china cap sieve

- Chop the dark chocolate, then melt over a bain-marie: the water should simmer, but not boil, and never come into contact with the chocolate in the bowl, otherwise the chocolate will become dull and lose its fluidity. (1). The temperature of the chocolate should reach 45°C on the cooking thermometer.

- When the temperature reaches 45°C, remove the bowl of chocolate from the bain-marie and place on the work surface. Leave to cool to 35°C, stirring occasionally. (2).

- Once the temperature has reached 35°C, position the china cap sieve above the chocolate and sprinkle with cocoa butter (3). Mix well then leave to cool to 31°C (4). It should be smooth and shiny.

- Test the chocolate to ensure it is well tempered and ready to use. (See p. 50.)

CHEF'S TIP

For milk and white chocolate, let the temperature drop to 34°C, then sprinkle with cocoa butter (1 % of the chocolate mass)

Tempering chocolate
by tabling on marble

Adjust the amount of dark chocolate used according to the recipe of your choice.

FOR 300 G OF TEMPERED CHOCOLATE

DIFFICULTY
Preparation time: 15 min

INGREDIENTS
300 g dark couverture chocolate 70%

EQUIPMENT
1 cooking thermometer • 1 large stainless steel spatula • 1 stainless steel palette knife

- Chop the dark chocolate, then melt over a bain-marie: the water should simmer, but not boil, and never come into contact with the chocolate in the bowl, otherwise the chocolate will become dull and lose its fluidity. (1). The temperature of the chocolate should reach 45°C on the cooking thermometer.
- When the temperature reaches 45°C, remove the bowl of chocolate from the bain-marie and pour three quarters onto the cold marble.
- Using the large stainless steel spatula, spread the chocolate out, from bottom to top and from left to right. (2) (3)
- Scrape the chocolate towards the centre with the large spatula, using the palette knife to scrape the chocolate off the large spatula. (4)
- Repeat the process (steps 3 and 4) several times to thicken the chocolate.
- When the chocolate begins to thicken, immediately return it to the bowl containing the remaining quarter of chocolate. Reheat it over the bain-marie, stirring gently (5), in several steps, to ensure the bowl does not overheat and rapidly raise the temperature of the chocolate. When the chocolate reaches a temperature of 32°C (maximum), remove immediately from the bain-marie. It should be smooth and shiny. (6).
- Test the chocolate to ensure it is well tempered and ready to use. (See p. 50)

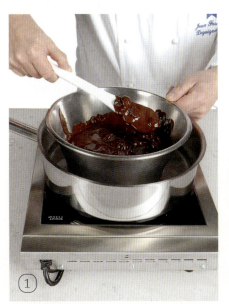
①

②

③

④

⑤

⑥

Checking the chocolate is tempered

- Pour a small amount of tempered chocolate onto a piece of aluminium foil (1).
- Leave the chocolate to set for 7 minutes in the refrigerator and peel off the foil. (2).
- If the piece of chocolate is smooth, shiny and breaks easily (3), the tempered chocolate is ready to use. If not, repeat the tempering steps.

Coating
chocolates

DIFFICULTY ♢
Preparation time: 45 min

INGREDIENTS
Ganache • Unsweetened cocoa powder • Couverture chocolate

EQUIPMENT
1 cooking thermometer • 1 round or tined dipping fork (optional)

- Prepare the ganache, shape it into balls. Leave to harden in the refrigerator according to the recipe of your choice (see, for example, p. 120, 124 or 228).
- Remove the ganache balls from the refrigerator. Allow them to return to room temperature (ideally between 18 and 22°C).
- Put the cocoa powder into a bowl.
- Temper a generous amount of chocolate (see pp. 45–48). Use a dipping fork or a normal fork (1).
- Slide the fork under a ball of ganache, dip it gently into the tempered chocolate, then take it out and leave the chocolate to drip over the bowl (2).
- Shake gently, then run the underside of the fork over the rim of the bowl several times to remove any excess chocolate and ensure a smooth coating.
- Use the fork to roll the chocolate ball in the cocoa powder (3). Leave to harden at room temperature for 10 minutes.
- As soon as all the chocolates have hardened, shake them in a sieve to remove the excess cocoa.

Moulding chocolates

DIFFICULTY ◯◯

Preparation time: 30 min • **Refrigeration time:** 40 min

INGREDIENTS
Couverture chocolate • Ganache

EQUIPMENT
1 cooking thermometer • Moulds of your choice • 2 piping bags • 1 wide stainless steel spatula • 1 soft acetate guitar sheet • 1 plastic dough scraper

- Temper the chocolate (see pp. 45–48), prepare the ganache and choose the moulds according to the recipe of your choice (see, for example, p. 132). Pour the chocolate and ganache into two separate piping bags.

- Pipe the tempered chocolate into the imprints (1).

- Immediately tap the mould on the work surface to remove any air bubbles, then turn it over and tap with a silicone spatula (2).

- Hold the mould upside down and scrape the surface of the mould with the wide stainless steel spatula (3). Only the sides of the moulds should be lined with chocolate. Leave to harden at room temperature for 10 minutes.

- Using a piping bag, fill the imprints with ganache, leaving a 2 mm gap between the ganache and the top of each imprint (so that it can be sealed), taking care not to overfill them (4). Leave to harden in the refrigerator for 20 minutes.

- Cover the filled imprints with a layer of tempered chocolate to completely enclose the chocolates with ganache and seal them (5).

- Immediately place the soft acetate guitar sheet on the mould, pressing down on each one to ensure the chocolates in the moulds are well coated (6).

- Scrape the surface of the mould with the plastic dough scraper to remove any excess chocolate (7), and leave to harden in the refrigerator for a further 20 minutes.

- As soon as the chocolates have hardened, carefully remove the soft acetate guitar sheet and turn the mould over onto the work surface, tapping it with a silicone spatula to unmould the chocolates (8).

- Set the chocolates aside according to the method and time indicated in the recipe.

Making paper cones for decorating

Adjust the quantity of chocolate or royal icing used according to the recipe of your choice (see, for example, p. 292).

DIFFICULTY

Preparation time: 5 min

INGREDIENTS

Tempered couverture chocolate (see pp. 45–48) or royal icing (see p. 282)

- Cut a 20 x 30 cm right-angled triangle from a sheet of baking parchment. Place your triangle with the right-angled corner at the top left-hand side. We'll call the right angle A, and the other two B and C.
- Roll angle B towards angle A to make a cone, forming a point on the longer side of the triangle (1).
- Then roll angle C over it to make the point of the cone as sharp as possible, and fold the tip of angle C inside the cone to secure it and prevent it from unrolling.
- Using a spoon, fill the cone a third full with warm tempered chocolate or royal icing (2).
- Close the cone by folding down the top part and rolling it downwards until the chocolate or royal icing accumulates in the tip of the cone. The paper should be taut. Cut the tip to the diameter you need and begin decorating (3).

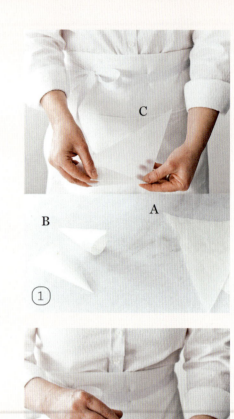

Decorating
chocolates

DIFFICULTY ♢

Preparation time: 25 min • **Refrigeration time:** 30 min

INGREDIENTS
Tempered couverture chocolate (see pp. 45–48) • Ganache

EQUIPMENT
1 chocolate transfer sheet • 1 dipping fork (optional)

- Make the chocolates according to your chosen recipe and place in the refrigerator to harden.

- Place the chocolate transfer sheet on the work surface. Take the chocolates out of the refrigerator and let them come to room temperature (ideally about 18 to 22°C). Use the dipping fork or a normal fork and slide it under the chocolate. Then, gently dip in the chocolate (1), lift it out and let the chocolate drip back into the bowl.

- Gently tap the fork on the rim of the bowl to let the chocolate drip off. Then, run the underside of the fork over the rim of the bowl several times to remove the excess chocolate and achieve an even coating (2). Place the coated chocolate on the transfer sheet and repeat the operation for all the chocolates.

- Leave the chocolates to harden in the refrigerator for 30 minutes, then peel them off the transfer sheet. Place the chocolates on a piece of card or baking parchment (3).

Making
chocolate Easter fish

DIFFICULTY ♙
Preparation time: 20 min • **Refrigeration time:** 20 min

INGREDIENTS
Tempered couverture chocolate (see pp. 45–48) • Coloured cocoa butter • Edible gold powder

EQUIPMENT
1 piping bag • 1 cooking thermometer • 1 pastry brush • 1 fish mould

- Pour the tempered chocolate into the piping bag.
- Melt a little coloured cocoa butter in a small saucepan to about 30°C. Place a sheet of baking parchment on the work surface. Brush the mould imprints with melted cocoa butter (1).
- Lightly sprinkle the imprints with gold powder (2).
- Pipe the tempered chocolate into the imprints (3).
- Gently tap the moulds on the work surface to remove any air bubbles, and leave to crystallise for 20 minutes in the refrigerator.
- Turn the moulds over onto the work surface to unmould (4).
- Chocolate fish will keep for up to 1 month in an airtight container at room temperature.

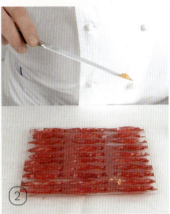

Confectionery classics

Mandarin fruit jellies

Brought back from the East during the Crusades, fruit jellies were probably created to preserve fruit so that it could be eaten out of season. For a long time limited to a few classic fruits, today the possibilities are endless, from traditional to tropical.

FOR 30 FRUIT JELLIES

DIFFICULTY
Preparation time: 30 min • Resting time: 4 h • Cooking time: 15 min

INGREDIENTS
16 g yellow pectin • 34 g sugar • 270 g mandarin purée • 56 ml mandarin liqueur • 250 g sugar • 110 g glucose • 9 g tartaric acid

- - -

Sugar for coating

EQUIPMENT
1 cooking thermometer • 1 x 4 cm Ø x 15 imprints silicone mould or 4 cm x 4 cm x 15 imprints

USING PECTIN

Yellow pectin sets slowly and is used for gelling ingredients which are rich in sugar and acids. It gives a fairly firm texture, allowing fruit jellies to hold well, while maintaining a certain elasticity specific to these confectionery products. Its properties cannot be reversed by heating, and it is also perfect for jams and jellied confectionery.

Mandarin fruit jellies

- Mix the yellow pectin and 34 g of sugar together.
- Warm the mandarin purée and mandarin liqueur to 40°C, checking with the cooking thermometer.
- Sprinkle the pectin-sugar mixture over the warm purée (1) and mix with a whisk. Bring to the boil, continue to cook for 5 minutes, then add the remaining sugar (250 g) and glucose.
- Continue cooking, stirring constantly with a silicone spatula until the temperature reaches 105°C (short thread) on the cooking thermometer. The consistency should be somewhat thick and heavy (2).
- Turn off the heat and add the tartaric acid, stirring in with a silicone spatula. Using a tablespoon carefully distribute the mixture into the imprints of the silicone mould (3). Leave to set for 4 hours at room temperature.
- Pour some sugar into a bowl. Turn the fruit jellies out of the mould (4) and roll in the sugar to coat them all over.
- Fruit jellies will keep for up to 1 month in a dry place in an airtight container.

Liquorice

Liquorice is a herbaceous perennial plant which has been used since ancient times by the Greeks and Romans. The rhizome is consumed in stick form and for making infusions, while the black paste, "liquorice juice", is the result of a very long extraction process and is used in syrups, powders, confectionery pastes, spiral sweets and alcohols. In confectionery, liquorice can be either hard or soft.

FOR 15 LIQUORICE PIECES

DIFFICULTY

Preparation time: 1 h • **Resting time:** 3 h • **Refrigeration time:** 30 min • **Cooking time:** 15 min

GELLING MIXTURE

25 g powdered gelatine • 250 ml cold water • 25 g cornflour • 25 g flour

- - -

90 g sugar cane molasses • 325 g unrefined raw sugar • 75 ml evaporated milk (unsweetened) • 175 g Trimoline® (inverted sugar) • 125 g butter • 2 g salt • 20 ml liquorice syrup • 20 ml pastis • 1 level teaspoon activated charcoal powder

Grapeseed oil for the mat

EQUIPMENT

1 cooking thermometer • 1 rigid piping bag • 1 x 10 mm Ø basket-weave piping nozzle • 1 silicone mat or 1 Silpain® mat

GELLING MIXTURE

- In a bowl, whisk the gelatine, water, cornflour and flour together. Cover the bowl with cling film and leave to swell in the refrigerator for 30 minutes.

- Place the molasses, unrefined raw sugar, evaporated milk, Trimoline®, butter and salt in a saucepan. Stir with a silicone spatula and bring to the boil. Add the gelling mixture and stir to melt.

- Continue cooking until the temperature reaches 115°C on the cooking thermometer. Add the liquorice syrup, pastis and charcoal powder and continue cooking until the temperature reaches 121°C (1).

- Carefully pour the mixture into a bowl. Leave to cool to 60°C, then pour into the piping bag fitted with the nozzle. Pipe 40 cm long strips on a baking tray lined with an oiled silicone mat (2).

- Leave to cool at room temperature for at least 3 hours or until the liquorice is no longer sticky to the touch.

- Trim the ends of the strips to make them straight, then roll them up (3).

- Liquorice will keep for up to 1 month in a dry place in an airtight container.

Ravioli sweets
filled with fruit jelly

These trompe-l'œil ravioli sweets will delight young and old alike with their original shape. The tropical, slightly tangy flavour of passion fruit pairs perfectly with the sweetness of the almond paste for a unique and surprising treat.

FOR 36 RAVIOLI SWEETS

DIFFICULTY

Preparation time: 1 h • Resting time: 15 h • Refrigeration time: 30 min • Cooking time: 30 min

CANDY SYRUP
1 litre water • 2.5 kg sugar

SUGAR SYRUP
100 ml water • 135 g sugar

PASSION FRUIT JELLY
175 g passion fruit purée • 5 g yellow pectin • 20 g sugar • 175 g sugar • 40 g glucose • 4 drops tartaric acid

RAVIOLI DOUGH
250 g almond paste (see p. 42) • 10 g butter • 10 g passion fruit purée • 3 drops liquid yellow food colouring

Cornflour • Icing sugar • Grapeseed oil for the mould • Melted cocoa butter for the dish

EQUIPMENT
1 x 14 x 30 cm mould for 36 ravioli • 1 cooking thermometer • 1 piping bag • 1 x 10 mm Ø plain nozzle • 1 stand mixer • 1 glass dish (or 1 candissoire tray) • 1 wire rack

Ravioli sweets filled with fruit jelly

CANDY SYRUP
- Prepare the candy syrup (see p. 39).

SUGAR SYRUP
- Pour the water and sugar into a clean, dry saucepan, stir to dissolve the sugar, then bring to the boil. Leave to cool.
- Brush the ravioli imprints with oil.

PASSION FRUIT JELLY
- Warm the passion fruit purée in a saucepan. Mix the pectin with the 20 g of sugar, then sprinkle it over the warm purée and whisk to combine. Bring to the boil, then add the remaining sugar (175 g) and glucose.
- Continue cooking until the temperature reaches 106°C on the thermometer, then remove from the heat and add the tartaric acid. Stir and pour into a bowl. Cover with cling film in direct contact with the mixture and leave to cool, then fill the piping bag fitted with the nozzle.

RAVIOLI DOUGH
- Prepare the almond paste.
- Put the almond paste, butter, purée and food colouring into the bowl of a mixer fitted with a paddle attachment and mix for about 5 minutes on low speed, until smooth.
- Take out the ravioli dough and divide it into two equal parts. Roll each part between 2 sheets of baking parchment dusted with a mixture of cornflour and icing sugar, and make two rectangles measuring approximately 20 x 40 cm x 2 mm thick. Carefully remove the paper, then place one sheet of dough over the ravioli mould (1). Take a small piece of the excess dough from around the mould and roll it into a small ball. Gently press the ball of dough into the imprints to hollow them out nicely, ensuring that the dough sticks to the mould.
- Brush the edges of the ravioli dough with the sugar syrup (2) as well as between each imprint.
- Pipe a small amount of fruit jelly into each imprint, so that it is slightly above the height of the mould (3). Trim the excess almond paste from around the mould.
- Using a rolling pin, carefully place the other sheet of ravioli dough over the mould to encase the fruit jelly (4).
- Press gently where the two sheets of dough meet so that they stick together. Seal with the top of the mould, then refrigerate for about 30 minutes.
- Carefully remove the sheet of ravioli from the mould, then use a small knife to cut along the lines to separate all the ravioli (5).
- Place the glass dish somewhere flat where it can stay undisturbed for 12 hours. Brush the base of the dish with a thin layer of cocoa butter. Place the ravioli in it without them touching each other. Cover completely with candy syrup so that it comes up to 1.5 cm above the ravioli (6), then cover with baking parchment in direct contact with the syrup.
- Leave the dish to stand for at least 12 hours at room temperature.
- Preheat the oven to 40°C. Tilt the dish to drain off the candy syrup. Slightly heat the base of the dish in the oven for 2 to 3 minutes to loosen the ravioli sweets. Place the ravioli on a wire rack over a baking tray and leave for a few hours, until the surface of the ravioli is completely dry to the touch.
- Ravioli sweets will keep for up to 2 or 3 weeks in an airtight container.

RASPBERRY RAVIOLI VARIATION
- These ravioli sweets can also be raspberry flavoured. To make them, replace the 175 g of passion fruit purée in the fruit jelly with 175 g of raspberry purée, and the 10 g of passion fruit purée in the ravioli dough with 10 g of raspberry purée. Change the colour of the liquid food colouring too: Use 4 drops of red food colouring instead of 3 drops of yellow.

Pink marshmallows

In the past, marshmallow roots were used to prepare this confectionery. Today, it is often made with sugar, glucose, egg whites and gelatine, to which a range of food colourings and flavourings (violet, poppy, etc.) can be added.

FOR 90 TO 100 MARSHMALLOWS

DIFFICULTY ♟

Preparation time: 45 min • **Resting time:** 24 h • **Refrigeration time:** 30 min • **Cooking time:** 7 min

INGREDIENTS

19 g gelatine powder 200 Bloom (or 9½ gold gelatine leaves) • 95 ml cold water • 65 g egg whites • 120 ml water • 395 g sugar • 50 g glucose • 10 g natural raspberry extract • 4 drops liquid raspberry red food colouring • 10 ml lemon juice • 35 g dried raspberry pieces (see p. 246) (optional)

- - -

150 g icing sugar • 150 g potato starch

Sunflower oil for the metal frame

EQUIPMENT

1 stand mixer • 1 cooking thermometer • 1 x 20 x 20 cm and 2 cm high metal frame

Pink marshmallows

THE DAY BEFORE

- Prepare the gelatine mass: Whisk the powdered gelatine with cold water in a bowl (if you are using gelatine leaves, make sure they are submerged in the water). Refrigerate for at least 30 minutes.
- Whisk the egg whites to soft peaks in the bowl of a stand mixer fitted with a whisk attachment.
- Pour the water and sugar into a saucepan, mix to dissolve the sugar, then add the glucose and cook until the temperature reaches 130°C (soft crack) on the thermometer. Remove from the heat and stir in the gelatine mass.
- Immediately and with care pour a thin stream of cooked sugar syrup into the whisked egg whites on slow speed (1), then increase the speed and whisk briskly for 5 minutes. Combine the natural raspberry extract, food colouring and lemon juice, add to the marshmallow (2). Continue whisking until the marshmallow has increased in volume and firm peaks cling to the tip of the whisk. (3). Slowly whisk in the dried raspberry pieces (optional).
- Combine the icing sugar and potato starch. Sprinkle part of the mixture onto a baking tray lined with baking parchment. Oil the metal frame and place on the baking tray. Tip in the marshmallow. Lightly oil a straight (icing) spatula and smooth the surface (4).
- Leave the marshmallow to set for 24 hours at room temperature.

ON THE DAY

- Sprinkle a baking tray with the remaining icing sugar/starch mixture.
- Turn the marshmallow onto a sheet of baking parchment, then remove the baking parchment from the surface.
- Remove the metal frame by running the blade of a knife inside the frame to loosen the marshmallow (5). Place the marshmallow in the icing sugar/starch mixture and turn to coat all sides.
- Cut into 2 cm wide strips (6), then into 2 cm cubes. Roll the cubes in the icing sugar/starch mixture, then sift to remove any excess.
- Store the pink marshmallows in an airtight container, they will keep for 1 week at room temperature.

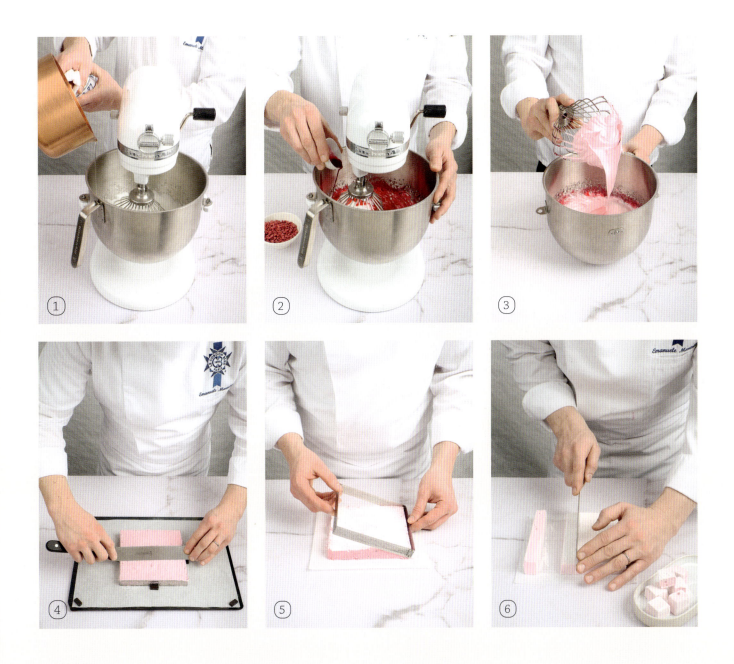

Soft nougat

Nougat is a confectionery made from sugar and honey and must contain 15% nuts. Its hard or soft consistency varies according to how it is cooked. Candied fruit can also be added. Several regions of France produce nougat, but Montélimar, once the capital of this confectionery, is the most famous nougat-producing town for its nougats containing at least 30% nuts, including almonds and pistachios.

FOR 30 SOFT NOUGATS

DIFFICULTY

Preparation time: 1 h • **Resting time:** 6 h • **Cooking time:** 15 min

NUTS
50 g whole hazelnuts • 190 g whole almonds • 50 g blanched pistachio nuts

MERINGUE
65 g egg whites • 60 g sugar

COOKED SUGAR SYRUP
50 ml water • 140 g sugar • 110 g glucose

- - -

1 vanilla pod • 140 g honey • 5 g cocoa butter • 2 sheets wafer paper

Grapeseed oil for the knife

EQUIPMENT
1 stand mixer • 1 cooking thermometer • 1 chef's blowtorch • 1 silicone mat
• 2 confectionery rulers • 1 serrated knife

COOKING HONEY

Cooking honey can be difficult for several reasons: its natural colour makes it difficult to distinguish when it is cooked, it cannot withstand cooking temperatures above 130°C, which causes it to burn, and the many impurities it contains cause it to foam when heated. The trick to solving all these problems is to heat it gently in a saucepan which is the right size for the quantity of honey, until it is coloured and cooked.

Soft nougat

NUTS

- Preheat the oven to 170°C. Place the hazelnuts, almonds and pistachios on a baking tray and roast for 10 minutes.

MERINGUE

- In the bowl of a stand mixer, whisk the egg whites until frothy, then increase the speed and continue until they are stiff and cling to the tip of the whisk. Add the sugar to stiffen the meringue.

COOKED SUGAR SYRUP

- Meanwhile, pour the water and sugar into a saucepan, stir to dissolve the sugar, then add the glucose. Heat until the temperature reaches 160°C (barley-coloured sugar) on the cooking thermometer. Carefully pour a thin stream of cooked sugar syrup into the stiff peak egg whites with the mixer still running (1) and continue whisking until obtaining a homogeneous consistency.

- At the same time, split the vanilla pod in half and scrape out the seeds with the tip of a knife. Heat the honey and vanilla seeds in a saucepan until the temperature reaches 130°C on the cooking thermometer. Immediately pour the vanilla-honey in a stream into the meringued egg whites and gently whisk.

- Replace the whisk with the paddle attachment (2) and mix on a slow speed. Using a blowtorch, heat the sides of the bowl while leaving the mixer running until of fairly firm and thick consistency (3).

- Melt the cocoa butter to 30°C, pour into the nougat mixture and stir.

- Add the nuts and mix gently at low speed (4).

ASSEMBLY

- Place a sheet of wafer paper on the silicone mat along with the 2 confectionery rulers, 1.5 cm high, and pour in the nougat.

- Using a rolling pin, roll out to the rulers and to a thickness of 1.5 cm. Place the second sheet of wafer paper on top and gently roll to seal (5).

- Leave to cool at room temperature for at least 6 hours. Using a lightly oiled serrated knife, cut into 2 cm wide strips, then into 5 cm long rectangles (6).

- Store the nougats for up to 1 month in an airtight container, or individually wrapped in cling film, away from humidity.

Hard nougat

In contrast to its famous cousin – soft nougat, which is very light and airy as it contains egg whites, and is made with cooked sugar and nuts – hard nougat, also known as black, red, Provence or crunchy nougat, is made with a dark cooked caramel to which almonds or hazelnuts are added.

FOR 12 BARS OF HARD NOUGAT

DIFFICULTY
Preparation time: 10 min • **Cooking time:** 20 min

INGREDIENTS
250 g whole raw almonds • 250 g sugar • 125 g honey

Grapeseed oil for the mat (or frame)

EQUIPMENT
4 confectionery rulers (or 1 x 18 x 18 cm stainless steel frame) • 1 silicone mat • 1 cooking thermometer • 1 serrated knife • Cellophane (optional)

CHEF'S TIP

Roasting almonds in the oven helps to remove any excess moisture and intensifies their flavour and colour. They become very crunchy with a delicious mouthfeel.

Hard nougat

- Preheat the oven to 170°C. Place the almonds on a baking tray and roast for 10 minutes.
- Position the confectionery rulers to form an 18 cm square that is 1 cm high on the lightly oiled silicone mat (or use an oiled frame).
- Heat a third of the sugar in a dry saucepan (1) to make a dark caramel. As soon as the caramel turns brown, add a second third of the sugar. Continue cooking, then, as soon as the caramel browns again, add the last third of the sugar and cook until it reaches a dark caramel (2).
- While making the caramel, heat the honey to 70°C in a saucepan.
- Stop the cooking process by carefully drizzling the hot honey into the caramel (3). Mix with a plastic spatula, then heat until the temperature reaches 155°C on the cooking thermometer.
- Add the roasted almonds and stir until they are all well coated with caramel (4), then immediately pour into the prepared square (5). Use a plastic spatula to spread to a thickness of 1 cm.
- Leave to harden until the nougat has almost cooled (about 10 to 15 minutes), then cut into 3 x 9 cm bars using the serrated knife (6).
- Wrap the hard nougat bars in cellophane (optional).
- Hard nougat will keep for up to 1 month in a dry place in an airtight container at room temperature.

Chocolate spread

Extremely popular, spreads are a staple for breakfast and for snacks.
As "homemade" spreads are increasingly fashionable, here's a recipe that's quick and easy to prepare. To make sure it's perfectly smooth, remember to stir it before using.

FOR 600 G OF SPREAD

DIFFICULTY
Preparation time: 10 min • **Cooking time:** 15 min

INGREDIENTS
½ vanilla pod • 250 ml cream • 15 g Trimoline® (inverted sugar) • 1 pinch fine "fleur de sel" sea salt • 75 g glucose • 175 g sugar • 20 g cocoa butter • 50 g milk couverture chocolate • 10 g butter

EQUIPMENT
1 cooking thermometer • 1 hand-held blender • 2 sterilised 300 ml jam jars

- Split the vanilla pod in half and scrape out the seeds with the tip of a knife. Heat the cream, Trimoline®, fine "fleur de sel" sea salt and vanilla seeds together to 80°C, then set aside.
- In another saucepan, cook the glucose and sugar without stirring too much to obtain a dark caramel. Stop the cooking process by carefully pouring in the hot cream mixture. Mix gently with a silicone spatula until smooth.
- Remove from the heat and add the cocoa butter, milk chocolate and butter. Blend with a hand-held blender until smooth, making sure that the blender head stays submerged – this avoids air getting in.
- Fill the sterilised jars and close them immediately.
- Chocolate spread will keep for 1 month at room temperature.

Chewy caramels
with fine "fleur de sel" sea salt

The word "caramel" describes the transformation that takes place when sugar is dehydrated when heated. A number of confectionery products are made with caramel, which can be hard or soft depending on how long they are cooked, the ingredients used and the production method.

FOR 60 CHEWY CARAMELS

DIFFICULTY

Preparation time: 1 h • **Resting time:** 2 h • **Cooking time:** 20 min

INGREDIENTS

250 ml cream • 1 vanilla pod, split lengthways and scraped • 190 g sugar • 175 g glucose • 15 g room-temperature butter • 3 g fine "fleur de sel" sea salt

EQUIPMENT

1 x 20 x 12.5 cm x 1.5 cm high (or edges of the same dimensions) stainless steel tray • 1 cooking thermometer • Cellophane paper or baking parchment

Chewy caramels with fine "fleur de sel" sea salt

- Line the base of the stainless steel tray with baking parchment.
- In a small saucepan, heat the cream with the vanilla (pod and seeds) until it boils. Set aside.
- Pour the sugar and glucose into another saucepan and heat to a dark caramel (180°C on the cooking thermometer) (1).
- Remove the vanilla pod from the cream, then carefully stop the caramel cooking by pouring in a small amount of hot cream. Whisk to combine. Whisk in the remaining cream in batches to prevent the caramel from setting.
- Whisk constantly to prevent the caramel sticking to the bottom of the pan (2). Cook the soft caramel until it reaches 120°C on the thermometer.
- Add the butter and fine "fleur de sel" sea salt (3), stir well, then carefully fill the stainless steel tray (4) and leave to cool to room temperature.
- When the caramel has set (about 2 hours), remove from the tray by running the blade of a knife around the inside edge, then tip onto a board covered with parchment paper (5) and carefully remove the paper.
- Using a large knife, cut out 2 cm squares (6), then wrap the soft caramels in cellophane paper or baking parchment.
- Store the chewy caramels at room temperature, away from moisture, for up to 3 weeks.

Hard coffee caramels

These flavoursome coffee-flavoured caramels will tantalise your taste buds. Elegant, yet very easy to make, they melt in your mouth. Share them with your family and friends by giving them as gifts on special occasions!

64 HARD CARAMELS

DIFFICULTY
Preparation time: 1 h • **Resting time:** 35 min • **Cooking time:** 20 min

INGREDIENTS
125 ml cream • 5 g instant coffee • 90 g sugar • 85 g glucose
• 12 g Trimoline® (inverted sugar) • 10 g butter

Grapeseed oil for the frame and spatula

EQUIPMENT
1 x 16 x 16 cm square frame • 1 silicone mat • 1 cooking thermometer
• 1 wide stainless steel spatula (or 1 large knife) • Cellophane (optional)

Hard coffee caramels

- Place the frame brushed with oil on a silicone mat.
- Pour the cream into a saucepan. Add the coffee and sugar. Bring to the boil, then add the glucose and Trimoline® (1) and cook until the temperature reaches 135°C on the cooking thermometer.
- Remove from the heat and carefully add the butter. Stir with a silicone spatula to stop the caramel cooking and make it smooth.
- Carefully pour the hot caramel quickly into the frame (2).
- Leave to cool for 5 minutes, then remove the frame. Using an oiled stainless steel spatula, deeply mark 2 cm wide bars (3), then make 2 cm squares or 5 cm rectangles.
- Leave the caramels to cool for around 30 minutes, then break them along the marked lines (4). Wrap the hard coffee caramels in cellophane (optional).
- Store for up to 3 weeks at room temperature in a dry place.

Candy canes

FOR 50 CANDY CANES

DIFFICULTY

Preparation time: 1 h • Cooking time: 30 min

INGREDIENTS

175 ml water • 500 g sugar • 1 tsp cream of tartar • 125 g glucose • 10 drops natural strawberry flavouring • 4 drops liquid red food colouring

EQUIPMENT

1 cooking thermometer • 2 silicone mats • 1 pair latex sugar work gloves • 1 sugar lamp

- Pour the water and sugar into a large saucepan, stir to dissolve the sugar, then add the cream of tartar. Heat until the temperature reaches 110°C (long thread) on the thermometer.

- Add the glucose and continue cooking over high heat until the temperature reaches 160°C (barley-coloured sugar). Add the natural strawberry flavouring.

- Carefully pour two thirds of the hot cooked sugar syrup onto one of the silicone mats.

- Add the red food colouring to the remaining cooked sugar in the saucepan and stir with the probe of the thermometer until evenly coloured. Carefully pour onto the other silicone mat.

- Leave the two quantities of cooked sugar to cool to about 80°C (the cooked sugar must stay malleable), then turn them over so they cool evenly.

- Put on the gloves, then take the outer edges of the uncoloured cooked sugar and fold them towards the centre. Roll the sugar into an elongated shape and place it under the sugar lamp. Repeat with the red cooked sugar.

- To give a satin finish to the cooked sugar, pull and fold it several times until you hear the sugar crackle (see p. 286). Put it back under the sugar lamp to keep the sugar hot and malleable.

ASSEMBLY

- Make a thick rope with the uncoloured satin finish sugar. Divide the red satin finish sugar into three parts and shape into ropes the same length as the uncoloured rope.

- Place the 3 red ropes alongside the uncoloured rope at equal distances. Roll them so that the red rope is incorporated and the rope is smooth. Stretch and roll the resulting rope to a thickness of 1 cm.

- Roll down with one hand and up with the other, without applying pressure, to twist the rope. Use scissors to cut 15 cm long sections, then immediately fold one end to form a hook. Leave the candy canes on a silicone mat to cool.

CHEF'S TIPS

To keep the cooked sugar syrup white, heat it quickly. Cooking it slowly will turn the syrup yellow.
• Use a fan to help cool the candy canes once they have formed.

Crystallised rose petals
and crystallised violets

CRYSTALLISED ROSE PETALS

FOR 100 PETALS

DIFFICULTY
Preparation time: 30 min • Resting time: 24 h

INGREDIENTS
10 fragrant organic roses • 2 egg whites • 1 pinch salt • 300 g fine sugar

EQUIPMENT
1 brush • 2 wire racks

- Remove the petals from the roses, keeping only the nicest.
- Beat the egg whites in a bowl with the salt to liquefy them. Pour the sugar into a bowl.
- Using the brush, apply a thin, even layer of egg white to both sides of each petal. Gently dip them in the sugar to coat both sides, and place them on the racks.
- Leave the rose petals to dry at room temperature in a dry place or in the oven at between 30 and 40°C for 24 hours, until they are completely dry.
- If properly dried, crystallised rose petals will keep for about 3 weeks in a large airtight container at room temperature.

CHEF'S TIP

Choose a fragrant variety of rose or violet as this will give a better flavour.

CRYSTALLISED VIOLETS

FOR 50 VIOLETS

DIFFICULTY
Preparation time: 25 min • Resting time: 12 or 13 h • Cooking time: 5 min

SWEETENED GUM ARABIC SOLUTION
100 ml mineral water • 35 g gum arabic powder • 25 g sugar

- - -

50 violets • Sugar

EQUIPMENT
1 hand-held blender • 1 fine-mesh sieve lined with muslin • 1 pair thin latex gloves

DAY 1
SWEETENED GUM ARABIC SOLUTION

- Bring the water to the boil in a saucepan, add the gum arabic combined with the sugar and bring to the boil.
- Blend using a hand-held blender, then set aside in a warm oven at between 35 and 40°C overnight for the gum arabic to dissolve completely.

DAY 2

- Spread the violets out on a dry cloth. Strain the gum arabic solution. Put the sugar into a bowl.
- With the gloves on, dip the violets one by one in the sweetened gum arabic solution, then in the sugar to coat them all over.
- Place the violets on a baking tray lined with baking parchment and dry for 2 or 3 hours in an oven preheated to 40°C.
- If properly dried, crystallised violets will keep for about 3 weeks in an airtight container at room temperature.

Filled barley sugar

FOR 500 G OF SWEETS

DIFFICULTY ✧✧✧
Preparation time: 3 h • Resting time: 1 h • Cooking time: 1 h

BLACKCURRANT FRUIT JELLY FILLING
8 g yellow pectin • 45 g sugar • 230 g blackcurrant purée • 90 g raspberry purée
• 330 g sugar • 65 g glucose • 5 g tartaric acid

PEANUT PRALINE FILLING
300 g shelled peanuts • 200 g sugar • 2 g fine "fleur de sel" sea salt • ½ vanilla pod, split and seeds scraped out

PULLED SUGAR
280 ml water • 500 g sugar • 350 g glucose • 5 drops tartaric acid • 3 drops violet liquid food colouring
(for the blackcurrants) or 3 drops orange liquid food colouring (for the praline)

EQUIPMENT
1 cooking thermometer • 1 piping bag • 1 food processor • 2 silicone mats • 1 sugar lamp
• 1 pair latex sugar work gloves • 1 pastry brush • 1 wide stainless steel spatula

BLACKCURRANT FRUIT JELLY FILLING

- Mix the yellow pectin and the 45 g of sugar together. Heat the blackcurrant and raspberry purées to 40°C.

- Sprinkle the pectin-sugar mixture over the warm purées. Bring to the boil and cook for 5 minutes, then add the 330 g of sugar and the glucose.

- Continue cooking, stirring continuously with a silicone spatula until the temperature reaches 105°C on the cooking thermometer. The consistency should be a little thick and heavy.

- Remove from the heat, stir in the tartaric acid with a silicone spatula, then pour into a bowl. Leave the fruit jelly to cool for 1 hour at room temperature.

- When cool, transfer the fruit jelly paste to the piping bag and leave at room temperature.

PEANUT PRALINE FILLING

- Preheat the oven to 170°C. Place the peanuts on a baking tray lined with baking parchment and bake for 10 minutes. Leave to cool on the baking tray.

- Put the sugar into a saucepan and dry-cook to a dark caramel (180°C). Pour the caramel over the peanuts and leave to cool at room temperature.

- When cool, break the peanut caramel into pieces and put in the food processor. Add the fleur de sel and vanilla seeds. Grind to a paste. Transfer the peanut praline to a piping bag and set aside at room temperature.

Filled barley sugar

PULLED SUGAR

- Pour the water and sugar into a saucepan and stir to dissolve the sugar. Bring to the boil and skim off any impurities with a skimmer or tablespoon. Add the glucose and heat until the temperature reaches 140°C (soft crack) on the cooking thermometer. Add the tartaric acid and heat rapidly until the temperature reaches 155°C (barley-coloured sugar).

- Carefully pour two thirds of the hot cooked sugar syrup onto one of the silicone mats.

- Add the food colouring (purple for the blackcurrant sweets, and orange for peanut praline sweets) to the saucepan with the remaining third of the cooked sugar syrup and stir with the probe of the thermometer until evenly coloured, then carefully pour onto the other silicone mat.

- Allow the two cooked sugar masses to cool to about 80°C (the cooked sugar should be malleable). Turn the sugar masses over so they cool evenly. Turn on the sugar lamp.

- Put on the gloves, then take the outer edges of the uncoloured cooked sugar first and fold them towards the centre. Then roll the cooked sugar into an elongated shape (rope) and place under the sugar lamp. Divide the coloured cooked sugar (purple or orange) into two parts: one third and two thirds, and repeat the operation with each piece.

- Pull the cooked sugar to make it shiny: take each end of the rope of uncoloured cooked sugar and pull it to a length of about 30 to 40 cm, then fold it in half. Repeat the operation about 20 times, until you hear the sugar crackle and the cooked sugar becomes opaque and white (see p. 286). Put it back under the sugar lamp to keep it warm and so that the satin finish white sugar stays malleable.

- Next, divide the satin finish white sugar in half, shape into ropes and put them back under the sugar lamp.

- Repeat the operation to make the two-thirds of the coloured rope shiny, then put it back under the sugar lamp.

ENCLOSE THE FILLING

- Using a clean rolling pin, roll out one of two pieces of satin finish white sugar to a 22 x 8 cm rectangle (1).

- Pipe a 2 cm thick by 20 cm long filling (blackcurrant jelly or peanut praline) down the centre of the satin finish sugar (2). Leave a wide space on each side so that the filling doesn't seep out when it has been enclosed. Lightly moisten the long edges with a wet brush, then fold the sugar over the filling so that the edges stick together. Press the rolling pin over the seam to seal in the filling (3). Roll to shape into a rope with an even thickness. Keep the resulting rope warm under the sugar lamp.

COOKED SUGAR RIBBON

- Divide the two-thirds piece of cooked coloured satin finish sugar in half and shape into elongated shapes the same thickness as the remaining satin finish white sugar. Roll the unpulled coloured cooked sugar into a rope of the same thickness.

- On the silicone mat, place side by side and touching each other: a satin finish coloured sugar rope; a satin finish uncoloured sugar rope; an unpulled coloured sugar rope; and a satin finish coloured sugar rope (4). Pull the sugar mass to lengthen it as evenly as possible. When it is about 30 cm long, fold it in half so that the inside edges meet, then stick the edges together. Repeat the operation two more times, then pull so that the ribbon is about 25 cm long and wide enough to wrap around the filled rope. Place the resulting ribbon on a silicone mat.

- Place the rope with the filling on the ribbon, then moisten it slightly before wrapping it completely in the ribbon (5). Gently roll into a nice, evenly rounded shape, then gently pull one end to form a 1 cm thick rope (6). Using both hands, roll one downwards and the other upwards to simultaneously and lightly twist the rope.

- Score the rope every 1 cm with a wide stainless steel spatula (7). When cool, snap it along the marks made with the spatula to obtain individual sweets (8).

- Filled barley sugars will keep for at least 1 month in an airtight container in a dry dark place.

CHEF'S TIP

Pay great attention to the temperature of the sugar: if it is too hot, the filling may seep out from the outer layer and the sugar will not be shiny. If the sugar is too cold, it will be difficult to shape the sweets.

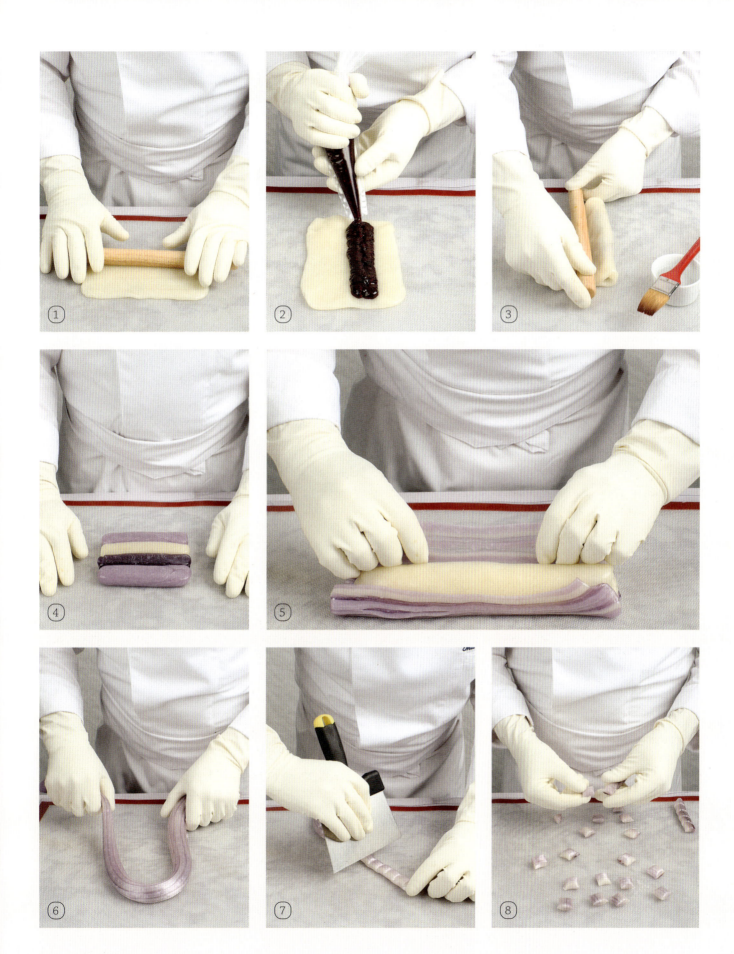

Liquid-centred sweets

A centre of cooked sugar syrup (with or without alcohol) is poured into moulds made from a mixture of starches. The starch, when in direct contact with the syrup, dries it out, forming a thin protective shell that keeps the syrup liquid inside. The centres are then dipped in candy syrup or chocolate to make very delicate sweets.

FOR 40 SWEETS

DIFFICULTY

Preparation time: 2 h • Resting time: 8 days • Cooking time: 15 min

STARCH TRAY

1.5 kg wheat starch • 1.5 kg cornflour

CANDY SYRUP

1 litre water • 2.5 kg sugar

COOKED SUGAR SYRUP WITH PEAR BRANDY

60 ml water • 135 g sugar • 62 ml pear brandy

Melted cocoa butter for the candissoire tray

EQUIPMENT

1 wooden box measuring 30 x 50 cm x 5 cm high, or 1 rimmed tray • 1 drum sieve • 1 flower stamp (or 2 cm Ø half-sphere) • 1 cooking thermometer • 1 jug • 1 dipping fork • 1 pastry brush • 1 candissoire tray (or 1 high-rimmed tray + 1 wire rack)

Liquid-centred sweets

DAY 1
- Prepare the starch tray (see p. 43).
- Press the flower stamp (or half-sphere) into the starch at regular intervals, leaving at least 1 cm between each one. Set aside the starch tray and 300 g of the starch mixture (to sift over the filled imprints), keeping both at a temperature of between 35 and 50°C.

DAY 4
- Prepare the candy syrup (see p. 39).

COOKED SUGAR SYRUP WITH PEAR BRANDY
- Pour the water and sugar into a saucepan, stir to dissolve the sugar, then cook until the temperature reaches 117°C (soft ball) on the cooking thermometer.
- Remove from the heat, add the pear brandy and cover immediately with a lid. Gently swirl the saucepan to combine the brandy and the cooked sugar syrup.
- Pour the cooked sugar syrup with pear brandy from one clean bowl into another about 7 or 8 times to lower the temperature to about 50°C.
- Place the warm starch tray on a flat work surface where it can be left undisturbed for about 24 hours.
- Pour the cooked sugar syrup with pear brandy into the jug and fill the imprints to the top (1).
- Sift a thick layer of starch mixture over the filled imprints (2).
- Leave to stand for 12 hours at room temperature.

DAY 5
- After 12 hours, carefully turn the pear brandy centres over using the dipping fork or your fingers (3) so that the sugar creates an even crust around them. Sift a layer of starch mixture over the top and leave to crust for about 12 hours.

DAY 6
- Using the dipping fork, carefully take the pear brandy centres out of the starch tray and place them on the rack (4).
- Use the brush to brush off any excess starch from the crust that has formed (5) (6).
- Place the candissoire tray on a surface where it will not be disturbed. Brush the bottom of the tray with a thin layer of melted cocoa butter. Gently place the pear brandy centres on the tray without them touching each other. Cover completely with candy syrup so that it comes up to 1.5 cm above the pear brandy centres then cover with baking parchment in direct contact with the syrup.
- Leave the tray to stand for at least two days at room temperature (depending on how thick you want the sugar coating to be).

DAY 8
- Preheat the oven to 40°C. Carefully pour off the candy syrup and place the sweets on a wire rack. Leave in the oven for 5 minutes to melt the cocoa butter. Use your fingers to gently pick up the liquid-centred sweets one by one by and place them on the wire rack. Leave to air dry for 4 to 5 hours.

CHEF'S TIPS

These pear brandy-filled sweets are very fragile and can break when turning them over or taking them out of the starch tray. • You can also dip the pear brandy fillings gently into tempered couverture chocolate instead of candying them.

Confit chestnuts
and candied chestnuts

Over 100 varieties of chestnut – commonly known as "marrons" in confectionery – exist in France, and each has a very different set of characteristics when it comes to size, texture, sweetness and colour. The Ardèche region is the best known in France for chestnut production. To make candied chestnuts, it is very important to use good quality chestnuts. Choose chestnuts that are nice and round, as well as a variety known for its sweetness, such as Bouche Rouge, Coutinelle or Marigoule.

CONFIT CHESTNUTS

FOR 650 G OF CHESTNUTS

DIFFICULTY

Preparation time: 3 h • Resting time: 3 to 12 h • Cooking time: 28 h

INGREDIENTS
500 g chestnuts, unpeeled • Salt

CONFIT SYRUP
1.1 litre water • 1 kg sugar cubes • 100 g glucose • 1 vanilla pod

EQUIPMENT
Gauze • Kitchen string • 1 cooking thermometer • 1 refractometer (optional)

CANDIED CHESTNUTS

FOR 16 CHESTNUTS

DIFFICULTY:

Preparation time: 10 min • Drying time: 30 min

CANDIED CHESTNUTS FROM ARDÈCHE
16 confit chestnuts in syrup • 400 g icing sugar • 90 ml water • 2 tsp confit syrup

EQUIPMENT
1 candissoire (or 1 tray with high sides) and 1 x 37 x 28 cm wire rack • Squares of silver metallic paper (optional)

CONFIT CHESTNUTS

COOKING THE CHESTNUTS
- Peel off the outer shell of the chestnuts (1). Bring a saucepan of water to the boil and submerge the chestnuts in it for at least 5 to 10 minutes. Using a skimmer, remove them one by one. Place in a cloth and, using a paring knife, peel off the skin while they are still warm (2). If the skin sticks, return the chestnut to the boiling water for 1 to 2 minutes, or until the skin comes off easily.
- Make little bundles of 3 to 5 chestnuts, tying them tightly in the gauze (3).
- Bring a large saucepan of lightly salted water (5 g per litre) to simmer at 90°C, and cook the chestnuts for 2 hours. Discard the water and repeat the operation for about another 2 hours. Check for doneness with the tip of a knife; the knife should go in easily (4).

CONFIT SYRUP
- Pour the water and sugar into a large saucepan and stir to dissolve the sugar. Add the glucose. Split the vanilla pod and scrape out the seeds with the tip of a knife and add to the saucepan. Bring to the boil, then add the gauze-wrapped chestnut bundles. Lower the temperature of the syrup to between 60 and 65°C, then confit the chestnuts for 24 hours. The water will gradually evaporate and the syrup will concentrate until it reaches 65° Brix on the refractometer (see p. 306).
- Leave the chestnuts to cool in the syrup. Drain the chestnuts from the syrup and carefully remove the gauze. Set aside in a covered container at room temperature.
- Confit chestnuts in their syrup will keep for up to 1 month in an airtight container.

CANDIED CHESTNUTS

- Drain the confit chestnuts and take 2 teaspoons of the confit syrup.
- Preheat the oven to 230°C. Prepare the candissoire tray topped with a rack. Place the chestnuts on the rack.
- Mix the icing sugar, water and syrup together in a saucepan. Pour a thick layer over the chestnuts to cover them completely (5). Place the tray and rack in the oven for a few seconds to allow the glaze to crust around the chestnuts. Remove the rack without moving the chestnuts (6) and leave to dry for 12 hours at room temperature or 3 hours in an oven preheated to 40°C.
- Wrap the candied chestnuts in silver paper (optional) and store for several weeks in a dry place at room temperature in an airtight container.

CHEF'S TIP

Confit chestnuts can be drained and used whole in desserts (e.g. chestnut charlotte) or broken up and added to cookie dough or cake batter.

Chocolate-coated
candied orange peel

FOR 30 TO 40 CANDIED ORANGE PEELS

DIFFICULTY
Preparation time: 30 min • Resting time: 20 min

INGREDIENTS
4 candied orange peel quarters (see p. 36) • 200 g dark couverture chocolate 70%

EQUIPMENT
1 sheet thick plastic or soft acetate guitar sheet • 1 cooking thermometer

- Use a sieve and drain the candied orange peel. Using a large knife, cut them lengthways into 5 or 6 mm wide strips (1).
- Place the plastic sheet on the work surface.
- Temper the chocolate (see pp. 45–48), then put it in a small bowl and dip the orange strips halfway into it, one by one (2). Hold each strip over the bowl briefly to drip.
- Run each chocolate-coated candied orange peel over the rim of the bowl to remove any excess chocolate, then place on the plastic sheet (3). Make sure the strips do not touch each other.
- Leave to harden for about 20 minutes before lifting the chocolate-coated candied orange peels from the plastic sheet.
- Chocolate-coated candied orange peels will keep for up to 4 weeks in a dry dark place at room temperature in an airtight container.

CHEF'S TIP

Make sure that the temperature of the chocolate does not fall more than 1°C below the tempering temperature. Keep a bain-marie on hand to warm it up for a few seconds if necessary, and stir the chocolate before using again.

Mendiants and chocolate buttons
with hundreds and thousands

MENDIANTS

FOR 50 MENDIANTS

DIFFICULTY

Preparation time: 15 min • **Resting time:** 30 min

INGREDIENTS

250 g dark couverture chocolate 70% • 40 g candied orange peel • 30 g roasted blanched almonds • 15 g sultanas • 15 g whole blanched pistachios

EQUIPMENT

1 cooking thermometer • 1 piping bag • 1 plain 4 mm Ø nozzle • 1 silicone mould 50 x 3.5 cm Ø round imprints

- Temper the dark chocolate (see pp. 45–48). Cut the candied orange peel into small pieces.

- Fill 1 piping bag with tempered chocolate, then pipe a layer about 5 mm thick into each imprint of the mould.

- Before the chocolate hardens, quickly arrange 1 roasted almond, 1 sultana, 1 piece of candied orange peel and 1 pistachio on each disc. Leave to harden for 30 minutes at room temperature, then store in an airtight container for up to 4 weeks.

CHOCOLATE BUTTONS WITH HUNDREDS AND THOUSANDS

FOR 60 BUTTONS

DIFFICULTY

Preparation time: 15 min • **Resting time:** 30 min

INGREDIENTS

250 g milk couverture chocolate • 50 g multicoloured hundreds and thousands

EQUIPMENT

1 cooking thermometer • 1 piping bag

- Line a baking tray with baking parchment. Temper the milk chocolate (see pp. 45–48).

- Pour the tempered milk chocolate into 1 piping bag. Cut off the end of the piping bag, then pipe small discs about 3 cm in diameter onto the baking tray.

- Before the chocolate hardens, quickly sprinkle each disc with multicoloured hundreds and thousands. Leave to harden for 30 minutes at room temperature, then set aside in an airtight container.

CHEF'S TIP

You can use other kinds of dried or candied fruit for the dark chocolate mendiants, for example: hazelnuts, walnuts, pecans, dried apricots, dried cranberries, dried figs, candied lemon or citron peel, crystallised ginger, etc.

Chocolate-coated almonds

FOR 600 G ALMONDS

DIFFICULTY
Preparation time: 30 min • **Cooking time:** 20 min

INGREDIENTS
400 g whole almonds • 1 tsp vanilla powder

COOKED SUGAR SYRUP
45 ml water • 130 g sugar

COATING
100 g dark couverture chocolate 70% • 15 g icing (powdered) sugar • 15 g unsweetened cocoa powder

EQUIPMENT
1 cooking thermometer • 1 drum sieve

- Preheat the oven to 170°C. Place the almonds on a baking tray and roast for 10 minutes, then leave to cool.

COOKED SUGAR SYRUP

- Pour the water and sugar into a large saucepan, stir to dissolve the sugar, then bring to the boil. Heat until the temperature reaches 115°C (feather) on the cooking thermometer.
- Add the almonds and vanilla, then stir with a rigid spatula until the almonds are well coated with the sugar.
- Carefully pour the almonds onto a baking tray lined with parchment paper, making sure they are well separated. Allow the almonds to cool to room temperature, then place in a large bowl.

COATING

- Temper the dark chocolate (see pp. 45–48). Pour the chocolate over the almonds in three or four batches and mix with a rigid spatula to coat them well, keeping them separate.
- Sift the icing sugar and cocoa together onto a baking tray, then position the chocolate coated almonds on top. Roll the almonds in the chocolate to coat well and leave to cool.
- Place the chocolate coated almonds in the drum sieve to remove the excess icing sugar and cocoa.
- Store the almonds for up to 4 weeks in an airtight container away from moisture and light.

Chocolate nougat

FOR 8 NOUGAT BARS

DIFFICULTY

Preparation time: 1 h • Resting time: 6 h • Cooking time: 15 min

NUTS
80 g pecan nuts • 80 g whole hazelnuts • 80 g whole almonds

MERINGUE
40 g egg whites • 20 g sugar

COOKED SUGAR SYRUP
30 ml water • 100 g sugar • 8 g glucose

- - -

½ vanilla pod • 125 g chestnut honey • 100 g dark couverture chocolate 70%
• 40 g pistachio nuts • 50 g unsweetened cocoa powder

Grapeseed oil for the metal frame and knife

EQUIPMENT
1 x 16 x 16 cm and 4.5 cm high metal frame • 1 silicone mat • 1 stand mixer
• 1 cooking thermometer • 1 chef's blowtorch • 1 serrated knife

- Oil the inside of the metal frame and place on the silicone mat.

NUTS

- Preheat the oven to 170°C. Place the pecan nuts, hazelnuts and almonds on a baking tray and bake for 10 minutes, then keep warm.

MERINGUE

- In the bowl of a stand mixer, whisk the egg whites until frothy, then increase the speed and continue until they are stiff and hold the tip of the whisk. Add the sugar to stiffen the meringue.

COOKED SUGAR SYRUP

- Pour the water and sugar into a saucepan, stir to dissolve the sugar, then add the glucose. Heat until the temperature reaches 160°C (barley-coloured sugar) on the cooking thermometer, while continuing to whisk the egg whites. Carefully pour a thin stream of cooked sugar syrup into the stiff peak egg whites and continue whisking until smooth.

- At the same time, split the vanilla pod in half and scrape out the seeds with the tip of a knife. Heat the honey and seeds in a saucepan until the temperature reaches 130°C. Pour the honey in a stream into the meringued egg whites and gently whisk to combine.

- Replace the whisk with the paddle attachment and mix on a slow speed. Using the blowtorch, heat the sides of the bowl while leaving the mixer running until a fairly firm and thick consistency is obtained.

- Melt the chocolate to 40°C and pour into the nougat mixture. Add the roasted nuts and pistachio nuts and mix gently at a slow speed.

- Pour the mixture into the metal frame and smooth the surface with a straight (icing) spatula. Leave to cool at room temperature for at least 6 hours.

- Remove the nougat from the metal frame by running the blade of a small knife around the inside edge and place on a chopping board. Sift the cocoa powder over the surface of the nougat.

- Using a lightly oiled serrated knife, cut into 2 x 16 cm bars.

- Store chocolate nougats for up to 3 weeks in an airtight container away from humidity.

Dark and milk chocolate truffles

The ganache used in this recipe is a preparation made with cream and melted chocolate. It is often used to make truffles or moulded chocolates.

DARK CHOCOLATE TRUFFLES

FOR 50 TRUFFLES

DIFFICULTY

Preparation time: 30 min • Resting time: 30 min • Refrigeration time: 1 h

DARK CHOCOLATE GANACHE

150 g room-temperature butter • 125 g fondant (see p. 40) • 200 g dark couverture chocolate 70% • 10 ml whisky • 5 ml coffee extract (or 18 g coffee paste) • 2 g bicarbonate of soda

COATING

250 g dark couverture chocolate 70% • 100 g unsweetened cocoa powder

EQUIPMENT

1 piping bag • 1 plain 12 mm Ø nozzle • 1 pair thin latex gloves • 1 cooking thermometer • 1 round dipping fork

MILK CHOCOLATE TRUFFLES

FOR 50 TRUFFLES

DIFFICULTY

Preparation time: 30 min • Resting time: 30 min • Refrigeration time: 1 h

MILK CHOCOLATE GANACHE

210 g milk couverture chocolate • 1 vanilla pod • 75 ml cream • 10 g glucose • 18 g room-temperature butter • 10 g Trimoline® (inverted sugar)

COATING

250 g milk couverture chocolate • 100 g chocolate sprinkles (or vermicelli)

EQUIPMENT

1 cooking thermometer • 1 piping bag • 1 plain 12 mm Ø nozzle • 1 pair thin latex gloves • 1 round dipping fork

DARK CHOCOLATE TRUFFLES

DARK CHOCOLATE GANACHE

- In a bowl, whisk the butter, adding the fondant a little at a time.
- Melt the dark chocolate over a bain-marie, then stir into the butter-fondant mixture. Add the whisky and gently whisk.
- Add the coffee extract (or coffee paste) and bicarbonate of soda, then continue to stir gently with a silicone spatula until smooth.
- Leave the ganache to thicken for 30 minutes, then place in the piping bag fitted with the nozzle.
- Pipe 2 cm diameter balls onto a baking tray lined with baking parchment. Refrigerate for 1 hour.
- Put on the gloves and roll each truffle between your hands until round.

COATING

- Temper the dark chocolate (see pp. 45–48). Sprinkle the cocoa onto a plate.
- Using the fork, dip the ganache balls one by one into the tempered chocolate, then immediately roll in cocoa powder. Leave to set in the cocoa for 5 minutes.
- Store the truffles for up to 15 days in an airtight container in a cool place (12°C maximum).

MILK CHOCOLATE TRUFFLES

MILK CHOCOLATE GANACHE

- Melt the milk chocolate over a bain-marie to 40°C. Split the vanilla pod in half and scrape out the seeds with the tip of a knife.
- In a saucepan, heat the cream, glucose and vanilla seeds to 60°C. Pour over the melted chocolate. Stir gently with a silicone spatula, then add the butter and Trimoline® and mix until smooth.
- Leave the ganache to thicken for 30 minutes, then place in the piping bag fitted with the nozzle.
- Pipe 2 cm diameter balls onto a baking tray lined with baking parchment. Refrigerate for 1 hour.
- Put on the gloves and roll each truffle between your hands until round.

COATING

- Temper the milk chocolate (see pp. 45–48). Sprinkle the sprinkles (or vermicelli) onto a plate.
- Using the fork, dip the ganache balls one by one into the tempered chocolate, then immediately roll in cocoa powder. Leave to set in the cocoa for 5 minutes.
- Store the truffles for up to 15 days in an airtight container in a cool place (12°C maximum).

CHEF'S TIP

Make sure that the temperature of the chocolate does not fall more than 1°C below the tempering temperature. Work with a bain-marie next to you to warm the chocolate for a few seconds if necessary and stir before using again.

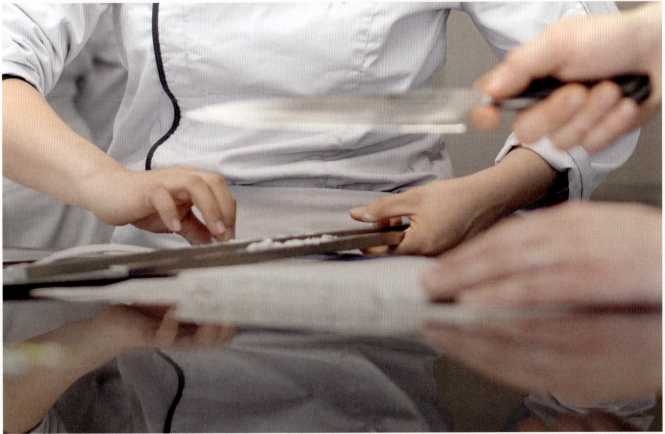

Chocolate praline rochers
and white chocolate coconut rochers

CHOCOLATE PRALINE ROCHERS

FOR 50 ROCHERS

DIFFICULTY ♛♛

Preparation time: 2 h • Freezing time: 1 h • Cooking time: 10 min

CHOCOLATE-HAZELNUT CENTRE
90 g milk couverture chocolate • 40 g white couverture chocolate • 225 g hazelnut paste

- - -

50 whole hazelnuts, roasted then skins removed (1 per rocher)

COATING
300 g milk couverture chocolate • 50 g chopped roasted almonds

EQUIPMENT
1 cooking thermometer • 1 piping bag • 1 Silikomart® silicone sphere lollipop mould with 67 imprints • 1 sheet silicone-coated baking parchment • 1 round dipping fork

WHITE CHOCOLATE COCONUT ROCHERS

FOR 30 ROCHERS

DIFFICULTY ♛♛

Preparation time: 2 h • Refrigeration time: 1 h 15 min • Cooking time: 20 min

CARAMELISED PEANUTS
160 g shelled peanuts • 18 ml water • 50 g sugar • 5 g butter

COCONUT GANACHE
240 g white couverture chocolate • 20 ml milk • 70 g coconut cream • 15 ml Malibu® • 25 g room-temperature butter • 20 g Trimoline® (inverted sugar, or honey)

COATING
400 g white couverture chocolate • 100 g desiccated coconut

EQUIPMENT
1 cooking thermometer • 1 piping bag • 1 x 10 mm Ø plain nozzle • 1 pair thin latex gloves • 1 round dipping fork

---

CHEF'S TIP

Make sure that the tempered milk chocolate stays at the correct temperature. If it falls below 29°C, put it over a bain-marie for a few seconds, then remove it, stir and check that the temperature has reached 29°C.

Chocolate praline rochers and white chocolate coconut rochers

CHOCOLATE PRALINE ROCHERS

CHOCOLATE-HAZELNUT CENTRES

- Melt the milk chocolate and white chocolate over a bain-marie to 40°C. Remove from the bain-marie, then add the hazelnut paste and mix well until the temperature drops to 24°C.

- Fill the pastry bag with the chocolate-hazelnut mixture, then fill the bottom of the silicone moulds to three-quarters full. Insert a whole hazelnut in the centre. (1). Close the mould (2), and fill to the top with the chocolate-hazelnut mixture (3). Freeze for 1 hour.

- Unmould the centres (4), and store in an airtight container at 15°C while you prepare the coating.

COATING

- Temper the milk chocolate (see pp. 45–48) and place it in a bowl. Prepare a dish with the chopped roasted almonds. Line a baking tray with baking parchment and place the sheet of silicone-coated baking parchment on the work surface.

- Using the fork, dip the chocolate-hazelnut centres one by one into the tempered milk chocolate, remove the excess by wiping against the edge of the bowl, then roll in the chopped almonds. (5). Place the chocolate praline rochers on a baking tray lined with baking parchment and leave to harden for about 15 minutes.

- Dip a second time in the tempered milk chocolate (6), then place the chocolate praline rocher on the sheet of silicone parchment paper and leave to set for about 15 minutes.

- Store the chocolate praline rochers for 1 week to 10 days at room temperature, away from moisture.

WHITE CHOCOLATE COCONUT ROCHERS

CARAMELISED PEANUTS

- Preheat the oven to 170°C. Place the peanuts on a baking tray and roast for 10 minutes, then leave to cool.

- Pour the water and sugar into a saucepan, stir to dissolve the sugar, then heat until the temperature reaches 115°C (grand soufflé) on the cooking thermometer.

- Add the peanuts to the cooked sugar syrup, then stir with a rigid spatula until they are well covered with white powder (sabler). Continue cooking until the sugar melts and a caramel forms around the peanuts.

- Add the butter, stir, then carefully pour the peanuts onto a baking tray lined with baking parchment, making sure they are well separated. Leave to cool to room temperature.

COCONUT GANACHE

- Melt the white chocolate over a bain-marie to 40°C.

- In a saucepan, heat the milk and coconut cream to 45°C, then pour over the melted chocolate. Stir gently with a silicone spatula, then add the Malibu®, butter and Trimoline®. Mix until smooth and homogeneous.

- Leave the ganache to thicken for 15 minutes in the refrigerator, then fill a piping bag fitted with a plain nozzle.

- On a baking tray lined with baking parchment, pipe 3 cm diameter balls. Place a caramelised peanut in each ball and refrigerate for 1 hour.

COATING

- Put on the gloves and roll each ball between your hands until round.

- Temper the white chocolate (see pp. 45–48). Put the coconut in a dish.

- Using the fork, dip the ganache balls one by one into the tempered chocolate, then immediately roll in the coconut. Leave to harden in the coconut for around 5 minutes.

- Store the white chocolate and coconut rochers in an airtight container at room temperature for 3 to 4 days.

Gold-flecked palettes

Created in Moulins, in the Auvergne-Rhône-Alpes region, by Bernard Sérady at the end of the 19th century, the gold-flecked palette is part of the local heritage and one of the pillars of the French chocolate industry. Made with a creamy ganache, a dark chocolate coating and gold leaf, this confectionery was an instant success.

FOR 36 GOLD-FLECKED PALETTES

DIFFICULTY

Preparation time: 2 h • **Chilling time:** 1 h 5 min • **Resting time:** 30 min

GANACHE
225 g dark couverture chocolate 70% • 1 vanilla pod • 270 ml cream • 30 g room-temperature butter

COATING
435 g dark couverture chocolate 70%

DECORATION
Edible gold leaf

EQUIPMENT
1 x 20 x 20 cm and 1 cm high frame • 2 x Rhodoïd® (acetate) sheets + 1 sheet cut into small 3.5 cm squares • 1 cooking thermometer • 1 plain 3 cm Ø biscuit cutter • 1 round dipping fork

- Cover the bottom of the frame with 1 Rhodoïd® (acetate) sheet.

GANACHE

- Melt the dark chocolate over a bain-marie to 40°C. Split the vanilla pod in half and scrape out the seeds with the tip of a knife.
- In a saucepan, heat the cream and vanilla seeds to 35°C, then pour over the melted chocolate. Stir gently with a silicone spatula, then add the room temperature butter and mix until smooth.
- Pour the ganache into the frame, smooth the surface with a spatula (2) and refrigerate for at least 1 hour.
- Run the blade of a knife around the inside of the frame, cover with a sheet of baking parchment, then carefully turn the frame over on the work surface.
- Temper the chocolate coating (see pp. 45–48). Once the ganache is cold, take 35 g of tempered dark chocolate and spread a very thin layer (chablonner) over the ganache using a spatula (3), then leave to harden.
- Cut out rounds using the plain biscuit cutter, (4), then refrigerate for 5 minutes.

COATING

- Using the dipping fork, dip the ganache rounds one by one into the tempered dark chocolate, and shake gently to remove any excess chocolate. Place them on the 2nd Rhodoïd® (acetate) sheet (5). Place a small square of Rhodoïd® (acetate) sheet on top (6) and leave to harden for 30 minutes at room temperature.
- Once the palettes have hardened, peel the Rhodoïd® (acetate) sheet off the palettes. Carefully decorate the surface of the palettes with a small piece of edible gold leaf.
- Store the palettes in an airtight container in a cool place (12°C maximum) and consume within a few days.

CHEF'S TIPS

If you don't have a plain biscuit cutter, use a knife to cut out squares.
- Make sure the temperature of the chocolate does not fall more than 1°C below the tempering temperature. Work with a bain-marie next to you to warm the chocolate for a few seconds if necessary and stir again before using.

Moulded passion fruit chocolates

FOR 48 MOULDED CHOCOLATES

DIFFICULTY

Preparation time: 30 min • Resting time: 8 h 30 min • Cooking time: 5 min

FOR THE MOULDS
20 g yellow coloured cocoa butter • Edible silver powder • 300 g milk couverture chocolate

GANACHE
200 g dark couverture chocolate 70% • 30 ml cream • 16 g sugar • 60 g passion fruit purée • 8 ml white rum • 15 g Trimoline® (inverted sugar) • 10 g softened butter

EQUIPMENT
1 pastry brush • 2 polycarbonate cocoa pod moulds with 24 imprints • 1 cooking thermometer • 1 piping bag • 1 soft acetate guitar sheet

PREPARE THE MOULDS

- Melt a little coloured cocoa butter in a small saucepan to about 30°C.
- Brush the mould imprints with the cocoa butter, then sprinkle with silver powder (see p. 57, steps 1 and 2). Temper the milk chocolate (see pp. 45–48), then pour it in to mould the imprints (see p. 52, steps 1 to 3).

GANACHE

- Put the dark chocolate in a bowl.
- Bring the cream, sugar and passion fruit purée to the boil in a saucepan, then pour over the chocolate. Stir in gently with a whisk.
- Stir in the rum and Trimoline®, then the butter. Stir gently with a silicone spatula until smooth. Leave the ganache to thicken for 30 minutes, then transfer to the piping bag.
- Fill the imprints with the ganache to within 2 mm of the top. Leave to harden for 4 hours at room temperature before filling the imprints completely with a thin layer of tempered milk chocolate. Immediately place the soft acetate guitar sheet on top and scrape off any excess chocolate (see p. 52, steps 4 to 8).
- Leave to harden for a further 4 hours at room temperature before unmoulding the chocolates.
- Moulded chocolates will keep for 1 week to 10 days in a dry place in an airtight container at room temperature.

CHEF'S TIP

Make sure that the temperature of the chocolate does not fall more than 1°C below the tempering temperature. Keep a bain-marie on hand to warm up the chocolate for a few seconds if necessary, and stir before using again.

Griottines® chocolates
and chocolate fondant cherries

The fondant inside these chocolates is transformed into an alcoholic syrup: the acidity of the cherry dissolves the fondant, forming a transparent liqueur. Enclosed by the surrounding chocolate, it creates a perfect balance with the fragrant, succulent cherry.

This is a variation on the Griottine® chocolates as here the stalks are left on the fondant cherries, giving them a delicate touch. Cherries can be replaced by other fruits, such as mirabelle plums in brandy.

GRIOTTINES® CHOCOLATES

FOR 28 GRIOTTINES® CHOCOLATES

DIFFICULTY

Preparation time: 30 min • Resting time: 5 h 30 min

INGREDIENTS
300 g dark couverture chocolate 70% • 50 g Griottines® in brandy • 100 g fondant (see p. 40)

EQUIPMENT
1 cooking thermometer • 1 pastry brush • 1 polycarbonate half-sphere mould with 28 3-cm Ø imprints • 1 piping bag • 1 soft acetate guitar sheet • 1 plastic dough scraper

CHOCOLATE FONDANT CHERRIES

FOR 15 CHOCOLATE FONDANT CHERRIES

DIFFICULTY

Preparation time: 30 min • Resting time: 1 h 45 min

INGREDIENTS
50 g pitted griotte cherries in brandy • 100 g fondant (see p. 40) • 250 g dark couverture chocolate 70%

EQUIPMENT
1 cooking thermometer • 1 Rhodoïd® (acetate) sheet (optional)

CHEF'S TIP

Make sure that the temperature of the chocolate does not fall more than 1°C below the tempering temperature. Keep a bain-marie on hand to warm up the chocolate for a few seconds if necessary, and stir before using again.

GRIOTTINES® CHOCOLATES

- Temper the dark chocolate (see pp. 45–48), then brush a thin layer into the mould imprints.

- Leave the Griottines® to drain for at least 1 hour. Set aside the brandy the cherries were macerated in.

- Cut each Griottine® in half and pat dry on kitchen paper.

- Place a half Griottine®, cut side up, into the centre of each imprint, making sure it does not touch the edge of the chocolate in the mould. Ensure that each Griottine® half is less than 3 mm from the top of the mould so that the imprint can be completely closed.

- Heat the fondant over a bain-marie to 60°C, then stir in 10 g of the reserved macerating brandy.

- Leave to cool to about 28°C, then transfer to the piping bag. Fill the moulds, leaving a 2 mm space between the fondant and the top of the mould (1).

- Leave to crust for 30 minutes at room temperature at about 18°C. When the fondant has hardened, seal the imprints with tempered dark couverture chocolate (2). Immediately place the soft acetate guitar sheet on top, and scrape off any excess chocolate with the plastic dough scraper (see p. 52, steps 6 to 8).

- Leave to harden for about 4 hours at room temperature before unmoulding the Griottines® chocolates.

- Store for up to 2 or 3 weeks in an airtight container at room temperature.

CHOCOLATE FONDANT CHERRIES

- Leave the cherries to drain for at least 1 hour, taking care that the stalks remain attached. Set aside the macerating brandy.

- Put the fondant and 2 teaspoons of the reserved brandy into a bowl. Heat over a bain-marie to 60°C.

- Dip the cherries in the flavoured fondant to coat them well. Let the excess drip off (3), then place the cherries on a plate or baking tray. Leave to dry at room temperature for about 10 to 15 minutes or until the fondant is no longer sticky to the touch.

- Temper the dark chocolate (see pp. 45–48).

- Check that the fondant around the cherries has hardened. Then, holding the stalk, dip each one into the chocolate and place on a Rhodoïd® (acetate) sheet or a plate (4).

- Leave the fondant cherries at room temperature for about 30 minutes, until the chocolate has hardened.

- Fondant cherries will keep for up to 3 weeks in a cool place in an airtight container.

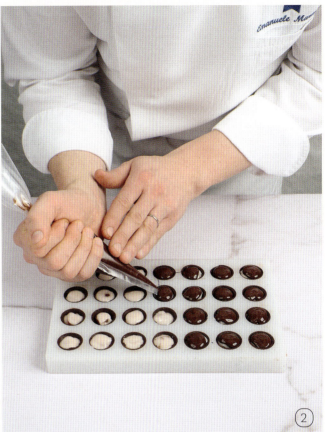

Filled chocolate
lollipops

Because they don't go soft and add crispiness and an original touch, crushed Gavottes® crêpes (wafers) – like those used in this recipe – have become a must-have ingredient in pastry-making. Using flexible, two-part silicone moulds ensures that the lollipops are easy to fill and perfectly spherical. A breeze to use, you can fill each half with a different filling for a more surprising experience when you bite into them!

FOR 20 LOLLIPOPS

DIFFICULTY

Preparation time: 2 h • Refrigeration time: 1 h 15 min • Freezing time: 2 h • Cooking time: 27 min

CHOCOLATE SWEET PASTRY
46 g flour • 10 g unsweetened cocoa powder • 25 g butter • 25 g sugar • ½ egg yolk

PRALINE CRISP
15 g milk couverture chocolate • 50 g almond-hazelnut praline • 40 g crushed Gavottes® crêpes (wafers)

CHOCOLATE GANACHE
30 g dark couverture chocolate • 75 g milk couverture chocolate • 75 ml cream • 15 g glucose • 15 g softened butter

COATING
200 g milk couverture chocolate

EQUIPMENT
1 x 2 cm Ø flower biscuit cutter • 2 Silpain® mats • 1 wire rack • 1 Silikomart® silicone sphere lollipop mould with 67 imprints • 1 piping bag • 1 plain 6-mm Ø nozzle • 20 x 10 cm long lollipop sticks

CHEF'S TIP

Make sure that the temperature of the chocolate does not fall more than 1°C below the tempering temperature. Keep a bain-marie on hand to warm up the chocolate for a few seconds if necessary, and stir before using again.

Filled chocolate lollipops

CHOCOLATE SWEET PASTRY

- Preheat the oven to 155°C.

- Sift the flour and cocoa powder together into a bowl. Add the butter, sugar and the ½ egg yolk. Mix with a plastic spatula until a dough begins to form. Transfer the mixture to the work surface and smear (fraser) with the palm of your hand, until a smooth dough comes together.

- Place the dough between 2 sheets of baking parchment and roll out to a thickness of 2 mm. Place on a baking tray and refrigerate for 30 minutes before cutting out flowers with a biscuit cutter. Carefully place the flowers on a baking tray lined with the Silpain® mat and cover with the other mat. Bake in the oven for 17 minutes, then leave to cool on the rack between the 2 mats.

PRALINE CRISP

- Melt the milk chocolate over a bain-marie, pour into a bowl, add the almond-hazelnut praline and the crushed Gavottes® crêpes and stir.

- Using a teaspoon, fill the lower part of the silicone mould (1), then smooth the surface with a plastic spatula. Leave the mould on a small tray in the refrigerator until hardened (about 30 minutes).

CHOCOLATE GANACHE

- Melt the dark and milk chocolates over a bain-marie to 50°C.

- Pour the cream and glucose into a saucepan, heat to 50°C, then pour over the chocolates and stir with a silicone spatula until smooth. Add the butter and mix until smooth.

- Transfer the ganache to the piping bag fitted with a nozzle.

- Place the top of the silicone mould onto the praline crisp, then pipe the ganache into the upper half-spheres (2).

- Leave in the refrigerator for 15 minutes, then insert a lollipop stick into each hole (3). Freeze for at least 2 hours.

- Keep the piping bag containing the remaining ganache for decoration at room temperature.

COATING

- Temper the milk chocolate (see pp. 45–48).

- Carefully unmould the lollipops (4). Dip them in the tempered chocolate (5), shaking gently to remove the excess chocolate, then place a chocolate sweet pastry flower on top of each lollipop (6). Stick the lollipops into a stand, such as a polystyrene one, and pipe a small dot of the reserved ganache in the centre of the flower.

- Leave the chocolate to harden for about 5 minutes.

- These filled chocolate lollipops will keep for 2 days at room temperature in their stand in an airtight container.

Regional Confectionery

Calissons

PROVENCE

This speciality from Aix-en-Provence dates back to the 17th century when they were distributed to worshippers during religious ceremonies to commemorate the plague of 1630. Now available all year round, calissons contain orange blossom water, honey, candied melon and candied orange peel – all ingredients typically associated with this region.

FOR 50 CALISSONS

DIFFICULTY

Preparation time: 1 h • Resting time: 13 to 15 h • Cooking time: 10 min

INGREDIENT

225 g blanched almonds

COOKED SUGAR SYRUP

45 ml water • 135 g sugar • 35 g glucose

- - -

10 g honey • 1 pinch salt • ½ vanilla pod, split and scraped • 135 g candied orange peel • 90 g candied melon • Zest of 1 lemon • Zest of 1 orange • 5 ml orange blossom water • 1 wafer sheet

ROYAL ICING

100 g icing sugar • 20 g egg white • 2 ml lemon juice • 2 ml distilled vinegar

EQUIPMENT

1 x 20 x 20 cm and 1 cm high frame • 1 silicone mat • 1 food processor

DAY 1

- Place the frame on the silicone mat. Place the almonds in a food processor and grind to a fine powder.

COOKED SUGAR SYRUP

- Pour the water and sugar into a saucepan, stir until the sugar dissolves, then add the glucose. Heat until the temperature reaches 120°C (firm ball). Carefully pour it over the almonds in the food processor and process for 2 minutes.
- Add the honey, salt, vanilla seeds, candied orange peel and candied melon cut into small pieces, zests and orange blossom water (1). Process for 5 minutes until smooth (2).

ASSEMBLY

- Pour the paste into the frame and use a spatula to smooth the surface (3).
- Cut the wafer sheet into a 20 cm square. Place it on top, then press well with a rolling pin to ensure it adheres (4).
- Leave to dry at room temperature for at least 12 hours.

DAY 2
ROYAL ICING

- Sift the icing sugar into a bowl. Add the egg white and whisk well. Add the lemon juice and distilled vinegar, then continue whisking until the texture is smooth and supple.
- Remove the dried calisson paste from the frame by running the blade of a small knife around the inside edge, then place it – wafer sheet side down – on baking parchment.
- Pour the royal icing over the calisson paste and, using a spatula, spread it evenly to a thickness of 1 mm (5).
- Leave the royal icing to dry for about 10 to 15 minutes, until it is no longer sticky to the touch. Then, using a large knife lightly moistened in cold water, score diamond shapes measuring 3.5 cm x 2 cm. Cut out the calissons (6).
- Leave the royal icing to dry completely for at least 3 hours at room temperature, or place the calissons on a wire rack and dry them in an oven preheated to 40°C for 1 hour. Leave to cool before serving.
- Calissons will keep in an airtight container at room temperature for 1 month.

CHEF'S TIP

To ensure a clean cut, wait for the royal icing to harden slightly before cutting the calissons into pieces, but don't let it harden completely before cutting them as it will become too brittle.

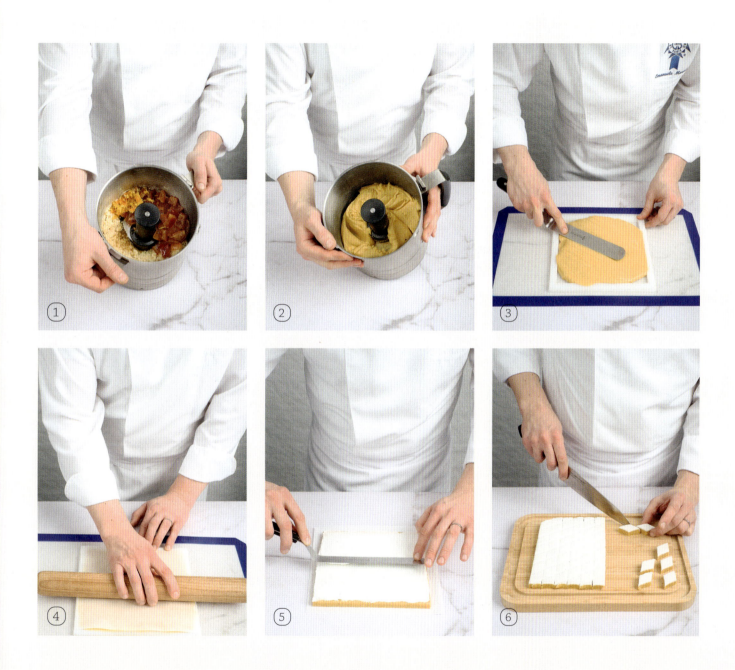

Pink pralines
LYON

A speciality of the Lyon region, pink praline was invented in the 19th century and is popular with gourmets the world over. Thanks to its colour, pink praline from Lyon takes us back to our childhood.

FOR 600 G PINK PRALINES

DIFFICULTY

Preparation time: 1 h • **Resting time:** 4 h (optional) • **Cooking time:** 40 min

INGREDIENTS

300 g whole almonds

COOKED SUGAR SYRUP

150 ml water • 300 g sugar • 5 drops liquid red food colouring

COATING (OPTIONAL)

25 ml grapeseed oil • 3 g beeswax

EQUIPMENT

1 copper syrup bowl • 1 cooking thermometer • 1 wire cake rack

CHEF'S TIPS

Copper is recommended for its heat-conducting properties. If necessary, use a stainless steel bowl. Coating the pralines helps to add shine and protects them from humidity.

Pink pralines

- Preheat the oven to 170°C. Place the almonds on a baking tray and roast for 10 minutes. Allow the almonds to cool to room temperature, then pour into the copper bowl.

COOKED SUGAR SYRUP

- Pour the water and sugar into a large saucepan, stir to dissolve the sugar, then add the food colouring. Heat to 118°C (soft ball) on the cooking thermometer.
- Carefully drizzle the sugar syrup over the almonds (1), then, using a rigid spatula, mix well to coat the almonds in the syrup and stir until they are covered in white powder (sabler) (2).
- Pour the almonds into a drum sieve over baking parchment to recuperate any excess sugar that has not coated the almonds. Return the almonds to the copper bowl.
- Pour the excess sugar into the pan. Heat to 118°C (if the sugar is too dry, feel free to add 2 tbsp of water to make it a little more liquid).
- Carefully pour the sugar syrup over the almonds and stir to continue coating them (3).
- Repeat the operation about 5 times, until the almonds are well coated with sugar and all the sugar has been used up.
- Pour the almonds onto a wire cake rack placed on a baking tray so that the excess sugar separates from the pink pralines and cool to room temperature (4).

COATING (OPTIONAL)

- Place the pink pralines in the copper bowl (or other bowl).
- Pour the oil and wax into a small saucepan over a low heat. Allow to melt, then pour over the pralines and stir with a rigid spatula to coat well.
- Place the pralines on a baking tray lined with parchment paper, then rest for at least 4 hours to allow the coating to dry thoroughly.
- Store the pink pralines in an airtight container for several weeks at room temperature.

①

②

③

④

Bergamotes from Nancy
and fizzy berlingots

BERGAMOTES FROM NANCY

FOR 30 BERGAMOTES

DIFFICULTY ⌒

Preparation time: 20 min • Cooking time: 10 min

COOKED SUGAR SYRUP

50 ml water • 175 g sugar • 25 g glucose

- - -

6 drops bergamot essence • 2 drops orange liquid food colouring

Grapeseed oil for the frame

EQUIPMENT

1 x 14 cm square stainless steel frame • 1 silicone mat • 1 cooking thermometer

FIZZY BERLINGOTS

FOR 100 BERLINGOTS

DIFFICULTY ⌒⌒

Preparation time: 45 min • Cooking time: 15 min

COOKED SUGAR SYRUP

90 ml water • 250 g sugar • 1 g cream of tartar • 60 g glucose

- - -

2 drops of green liquid food colouring • 2 drops of lime flavouring

- - -

2 g citric acid powder • 2 g bicarbonate of soda

EQUIPMENT

1 cooking thermometer • 1 silicone mat • 1 pair latex sugar work gloves • 1 sugar lamp

---

CHEF'S TIP

Citric acid and bicarbonate of soda are what give the berlingots their fizziness.

BERGAMOTES FROM NANCY

- Brush the frame with the oil, then place it on a baking tray lined with the silicone mat.

COOKED SUGAR SYRUP

- Pour the water and sugar into a saucepan and stir to dissolve the sugar. Add the glucose, bring to the boil, then skim off any impurities with a skimmer or tablespoon. Continue cooking until the temperature reaches 150°C (sugar light yellow) on the cooking thermometer.

- Remove from the heat and add the bergamot essence and orange food colouring. Stir with the probe of the thermometer until evenly coloured, then carefully pour into the frame.

- When the temperature has dropped to 60°C, remove the frame and, using a large knife, score 2 cm wide strips in the cooked sugar. Do the same in the other direction to make 2 x 2 cm squares and leave to cool.

- Break the cooked sugar along the scored marks to obtain the bergamotes from Nancy.

- Bergamotes from Nancy will keep for up to 4 weeks in a dry place in an airtight container.

FIZZY BERLINGOTS

COOKED SUGAR SYRUP

- Pour the water, sugar and cream of tartar into a saucepan and stir to dissolve the sugar and cream of tartar. Bring to the boil and skim off any impurities with a skimmer or tablespoon. Cook until the temperature reaches 110°C (thread) on the cooking thermometer. Add the glucose and continue cooking over high heat until the temperature reaches 160°C (barley-coloured sugar).

- Add the food colouring and flavouring and stir with the probe of the thermometer until evenly coloured.

- Carefully pour onto the silicone mat, leave to cool to 80°C, then sprinkle the coloured cooked sugar with the citric acid. Fold the sugar to cover the acid, then sprinkle with bicarbonate of soda and fold again.

- Put on the gloves and remove a quarter of the mass of cooked sugar. Shape the remaining three quarters into a rope, turn it over so it cools evenly and place it under the lamp (the cooked sugar must remain malleable).

- Take the outer edges of the first quarter of the cooked sugar mass and bring them towards the centre. Roll the sugar into a rope. Place the resulting sugar under a sugar lamp to prevent it from cooling.

- Pull the cooked sugar to give a satin finish: take each end of the cooked sugar rope and stretch to a length of about 30 to 40 cm, then fold it in half. Repeat the operation about 20 times until you hear the sugar crackle and the cooked sugar is opaque (see p. 286).

ASSEMBLY

- When the sugar has a satin finish, pull it into a thin rope, then cut it to the length of the three quarters of cooked sugar. Stick the ropes to the large rope at regular intervals, turning the rope to give a zebra-stripe effect.

- Roll together to form a long rope, 1 to 1.5 cm in diameter.

- Use scissors to cut into berlingots, turning the rope a quarter turn between each cut. To cool them quickly, place the berlingots well apart on a wire rack lined with baking parchment.

- Fizzy berlingots will keep for up to 4 weeks in a dry place in an airtight container.

Apple sweets

NORMANDY

Dating back to the 17th century, apple sweets were made with apple juice until the mid-19th century. Since then, they have been made with natural apple extract.
Apple sweets originally came in a variety of forms: tablets, lozenges, etc., but it is the cylindrical shape that has become famous.

FOR 20 APPLE SWEETS

DIFFICULTY

Preparation time: 55 min • Cooking time: 10 min

INGREDIENTS

80 ml apple juice • 70 ml dry cider • 250 g sugar • 1 g citric acid • 5 drops natural apple flavouring • Icing sugar

EQUIPMENT

1 cooking thermometer • 1 silicone mat • 1 pair latex sugar work gloves • 1 sugar lamp (optional) • Gold foil

- Pour the apple juice, cider and sugar into a saucepan, stir to dissolve the sugar, then heat until the temperature reaches 148°C on the cooking thermometer.
- Remove from the heat and add the citric acid and natural apple flavouring. Carefully pour onto the silicone mat.
- Leave the cooked sugar mass to cool to about 80°C (the cooked sugar must remain malleable). Turn the mixture over so that it cools evenly.
- Put on the gloves and bring the outer edges of the sugar towards the middle. Then roll the sugar into a rope.
- To give the cooked sugar a satin finish, pull and fold it several times until you hear the sugar crackle (see p. 286).
- Shape into a 1.5 cm diameter rope, then cut into 10 cm long batons. If the sugar becomes too hard to cut, place it briefly under the sugar lamp.
- Leave the apple sweets to cool on the silicone mat, then roll them in icing sugar to protect them from moisture. Wrap each apple sweet in a square of foil.
- They will keep for up to 3 to 4 weeks in a dry place in an airtight container.

Mirabelles from Lorraine

This little plum is a speciality of Lorraine, which produces between 70 and 80% of the world's supply. Harvested from August to September, mirabelle plums have a short season. They are eaten fresh, in syrup or in brandy. The brandy produced in Lorraine has been awarded a regulated designation of origin.

FOR 30 MIRABELLES

DIFFICULTY ○○○

Preparation time: 1 h 30 min • **Resting time:** 5 days • **Cooking time:** 10 min

STARCH TRAY
1.5 kg wheat starch • 1.5 kg cornflour

MIRABELLE PLUM BRANDY CENTRES
100 ml mineral water • 250 g sugar cubes • 75 ml mirabelle plum brandy

COATING
250 g white couverture chocolate

MIRABELLE ALMOND PASTE
300 g almond paste (see p. 42) • 15 ml mirabelle plum brandy
• Orange liquid food colouring • Red liquid food colouring

Icing sugar for sprinkling

FINISH
1 or 2 drops of red liquid food colouring • 50 ml sugar syrup (see p. 32) or 50 ml mirabelle plum brandy

EQUIPMENT
1 wooden box measuring 30 x 50 cm x 5 cm high, or 1 rimmed tray • 1 half-sphere mould 2 cm in diameter • 1 cooking thermometer • 1 jug • 1 drum sieve • 1 pastry brush • 1 dipping fork • 1 soft acetate guitar sheet • 1 silicone mat • 1 fine brush

DAY 1
STARCH TRAY
- Prepare the starch tray (see p. 43).
- Make half-sphere indentations in the starch at regular intervals, leaving at least 1 cm between each one. Set aside the starch tray and 300 g of the starch mixture (to sift over the filled indents), keeping both at a temperature of between 35 and 50°C.

DAY 4
MIRABELLE PLUM BRANDY CENTRES
- Pour the water and sugar into a saucepan, stir to dissolve the sugar, then cook until the temperature reaches 120°C (firm ball) on the cooking thermometer. Remove from the heat, leave to cool for 2 minutes, then add the mirabelle plum brandy.
- Place the warm starch tray on a flat work surface where it can be left undisturbed for about 22 hours.
- Pour the syrup from one bowl into another 4 to 6 times to obtain a homogeneous mixture. Pour the mixture into the jug and carefully fill the indentations to the top.
- Mix the 300 g of reserved starch and sift a thick layer over the filled indents. Set aside at 35 to 40°C for at least 6 hours, then carefully turn the centres out using a spoon. Sift a layer of starch mixture over them and leave to crust for a further 4 hours at 35 to 40°C, then at room temperature for 12 hours.

DAY 5
- Gently brush the starch layer off the top of the mirabelle plum brandy centres. Then, use a spoon to remove them one by one while brushing them. Carefully place the centres on a plate.

COATING
- Temper the white chocolate (see pp. 45–48).
- Using the dipping fork, dip the mirabelle plum brandy centres into the white chocolate (1). Let the excess chocolate drip back into the bowl. Run each centre over the rim of the bowl to remove any excess chocolate, then set aside at room temperature on the soft acetate guitar sheet until completely hardened (about 1 hour).

MIRABELLE ALMOND PASTE
- Prepare the almond paste.
- Dust the silicone mat with icing sugar and work the almond paste with the palm of your hand to soften it. Add the mirabelle plum brandy, then a few drops of orange food colouring and continue working the dough until it is evenly coloured.
- Shape into a rope about 2 to 3 cm thick, then cut it into 30 pieces. Roll each piece into a ball. Flatten the balls of almond paste to a thickness of 2 mm and a diameter of about 5 cm. Dust with icing sugar if the almond paste starts to stick to the silicone mat.
- Place a chocolate-covered mirabelle plum brandy centre in the middle of each almond paste disc (2) then gently fold the paste around it to form a smooth ball (3). Place the mirabelles on the silicone mat.

FINISH
- Pour the red colouring and sugar syrup or mirabelle plum brandy into a small bowl and mix well. Using the fine brush, delicately paint a few spots on the surface of the mirabelles (4). Leave to dry for about 30 minutes, then turn them over and paint the other side. Leave to dry for about 30 minutes.
- Take a small amount of the remaining almond paste, add a knife tip of red food colouring, then roll into very thin strands to make the stems of the plums.
- Make a small depression in the top of each mirabelle and attach a stem to it. Using the edge of a ruler, score a line from the stem to the base of each mirabelle.
- Mirabelles will keep for up to 3 or 4 weeks in a dry place in an airtight container.

Nougatines
de Nevers

Nougatines de Nevers, with their pretty orange coating, were created in 1850 by Jean-Louis Bourumeau, a confectioner from the region of the same name. They have since become one of the city's iconic gourmet products. Their popularity is mainly due to an official visit by Napoleon III in 1862, during which Empress Eugénie was treated to this confectionery: she went on to order these nougatines, introducing them to the Parisian glitterati of the day.

FOR 35 NOUGATINES

DIFFICULTY

Preparation time: 45 min • Resting time: 5 h 25 min • Cooking time: 15 min

NOUGATINE
60 g chopped almonds • 10 g butter

COOKED SUGAR SYRUP
22 ml water • 28 g sugar • 85 g glucose

ORANGE COATING
90 g egg whites • 300 g icing sugar • Orange food colouring powder

EQUIPMENT
1 cooking thermometer • 1 silicone mat • 1 Silikomart® micro round stone mould with 35 imprints • 1 stand mixer • 1 round dipping fork • 1 rack • 1 dehydrator (optional)

- Preheat the oven to 170°C. Place the chopped almonds on a baking tray and roast for 10 minutes, then leave to cool.

COOKED SUGAR SYRUP

- Pour the water and sugar into a saucepan, stir until the sugar dissolves, then add the glucose. Heat until the temperature reaches 170°C (caramel) on the cooking thermometer.

NOUGATINE

- Add the chopped roasted almonds and butter to the cooked sugar syrup, then stir with a silicone spatula until the almonds are coated. Pour the preparation onto the silicone mat and leave to cool until thickened.

- While the nougatine is still warm, shape into 3 ropes 1 cm in diameter. Using scissors, cut the ropes into 2 cm long pieces, then mould them into the imprints of the silicone mould, pressing lightly with your fingers (1).

- Leave the nougatines to harden for 10 minutes at room temperature, then unmould and place on a sheet of baking parchment.

ORANGE COATING

- In the bowl of the mixer fitted with a whisk attachment, beat the egg whites, icing sugar and a knife tip of orange food colouring until the mixture is frothy and smooth (2). Pour into a bowl.

- Using the dipping fork, dip the nougatines one by one on one side, remove the excess coating, then place them, undipped side down, on the rack to dry (3). Place the rack in a dehydrator or put in the oven at between 35 and 40°C for 1 hour.

- When the first coating has dried, repeat the operation on the other side (4). Place the nougatines de Nevers on the rack and leave to dry for 4 hours at 35 to 40°C.

- Nougatines de Nevers will keep for up to 1 month in a dry place in an airtight container.

CHEF'S TIPS

Add 35 g of cocoa paste at the end of cooking the nougatine to make chocolate nougatines de Nevers.
• Put the silicone mould with the nougatines in a 110°C oven for about 10 minutes, so that they take the shape of the mould nicely. • Work the nougatine on a hot tray so that it doesn't harden too quickly.

Coussins de Lyon

In 1960, a chocolatier by the name of Voisin was inspired by a historical event to create this emblematic Lyon confectionery, shaped to look like a silk cushion. In 1643, the city of Lyon was ravaged by a plague, so the authorities organised a huge procession to go to Fourvière Hill to ask the Virgin to help them. A candle weighing over 3 kg and a golden shield on a silk cushion were placed at the foot of the statue, and a promise was made: if the town was saved, that same pilgrimage would be made every year.

FOR 36 COUSSINS DE LYON

DIFFICULTY

Preparation time: 30 to 45 min • Resting time: 24 h • Cooking time: 5 min

CURAÇAO GANACHE

135 g dark couverture chocolate 70% • 95 ml cream • 5 g Trimoline® (inverted sugar) • 18 g softened butter • 5 ml curaçao

ALMOND PASTE

400 g almond paste (see p. 42) • Blue liquid food colouring • Green liquid food colouring

Icing sugar for sprinkling

FINISH

Curaçao • White granulated sugar

EQUIPMENT

1 x 14 x 14 cm and 0.8 cm high stainless steel frame • 1 cooking thermometer • 2 soft acetate guitar sheets • 1 small wooden stick • 1 pastry brush

Coussins de Lyon

DAY 1
CURAÇAO GANACHE

- Line the base of the frame with a sheet of baking parchment or a soft acetate guitar sheet.
- Melt the dark chocolate over a bain-marie, making sure it does not exceed 50°C.
- In a saucepan, heat the cream to 60°C. Pour the cream over the melted chocolate in three batches, stirring with a silicone spatula and taking care not to incorporate any air.
- Next, add the Trimoline® and butter, stirring until incorporated, then add the curaçao and stir well. Pour the ganache into the frame and use a spatula to smooth the surface. Set aside at room temperature in a dry place for 24 hours.

DAY 2

- The next day, remove the curaçao ganache from the frame by running the blade of a small knife around the inside edge, then place it on baking parchment on a chopping board. Using a large knife, cut into six 2 cm wide strips. Leave the strips on the board (1).

ALMOND PASTE

- Prepare the almond paste.
- Dust the work surface with icing sugar and knead the almond paste to soften it. Add a few drops of the blue and green food colouring and continue working the dough until it is smooth and as bright in colour as desired.
- Take about 60 g of almond paste for the middle strip, then add 1 to 2 drops of blue food colouring to intensify the colour. Roll out to a 24 cm long x 2 mm thick strip. Cut into six strips approximately 5 mm wide.
- Roll the remaining almond paste out between 2 soft acetate guitar sheets – sprinkled with icing sugar – into a rectangle measuring 36 x 16 cm x 2 mm thick.
- Cut into six 6 x 16 cm strips (2). Press a wooden stick down the middle of the rectangle to lightly mark a line and place a thin strip of blue almond paste along it (3). Use the rolling pin to gently incorporate the blue almond paste into the green one, then turn it over.
- Using a small spatula, place a strip of ganache down the centre of each blue and green almond paste rectangle (4). Wrap the ganache with the almond paste (5) and press well to seal.
- Lightly brush the resulting strips with curaçao, then sprinkle with granulated sugar to cover completely. Cut off the ends where there is no ganache filling, then cut 2.5 cm squares from the trimmed strips (6).
- Coussins de Lyon will keep for up to 10 days in an airtight container at room temperature.

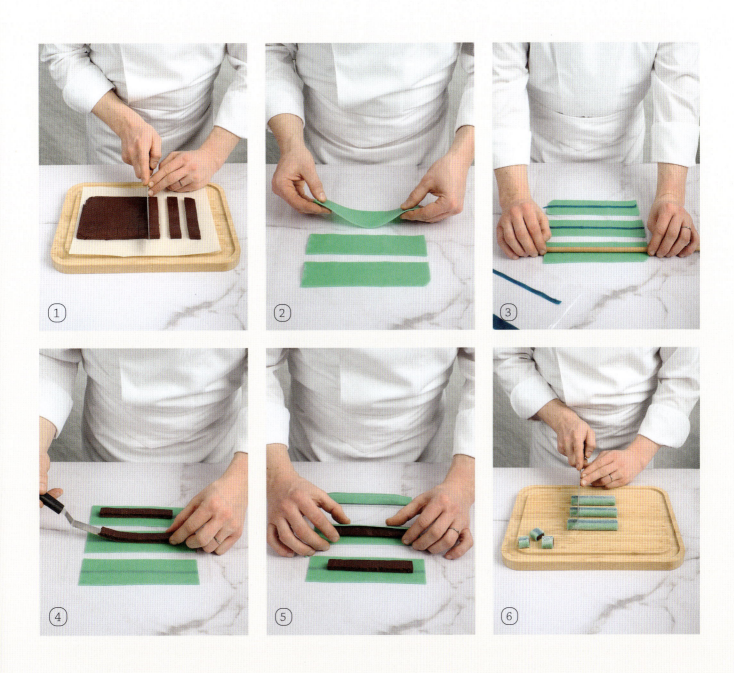

Caprices

AGEN

The reddish-purple oval Ente plum is the only variety used to make Agen prunes and has been awarded PGI status. Caprices were created in 1964 by the Coufidou cooperative, specifically using Agen's iconic prunes.

FOR 15 CAPRICES

DIFFICULTY

Preparation time: 1 h 15 min • **Refrigeration time:** 5 to 10 min • **Resting time:** 30 min • **Cooking time:** 30 min

NOUGATINE
60 g chopped almonds • 10 g butter

COOKED SUGAR SYRUP
22 ml water • 85 g sugar • 85 g glucose

PRUNE CREAM
200 g pitted prunes • 2 g NH pectin • 133 g sugar • 100 ml water • 15 g honey • 2 g lemon zest
• ½ vanilla pod, split and seeds scraped out

FINISH
70 g small walnut kernels • 150 g dark couverture chocolate 70%

EQUIPMENT
1 cooking thermometer • 2 silicone mats • 1 x 3.5 cm Ø biscuit cutter • 1 x 4 cm Ø x 15 mm polycarbonate half-sphere mould • 1 food processor • 1 piping bag • 1 plain 10 mm Ø nozzle • 1 Rhodoïd® (acetate) sheet • 1 round dipping fork

USING NH PECTIN

NH pectin reacts in a sweet, acidic environment and results in a firm, glossy texture. A coating made with this pectin is reversible and can withstand several successive gelling and remelting operations while retaining its properties.

Caprices

- Preheat the oven to 170°C. Place the chopped almonds on a baking tray and roast for 10 minutes.

COOKED SUGAR SYRUP

- Pour the water and sugar into a saucepan, stir until the sugar dissolves, then add the glucose. Heat until the temperature reaches 170°C (caramel).

NOUGATINE

- Add the chopped roasted almonds and butter to the cooked sugar syrup, then mix with a silicone spatula to coat the almonds. Pour the nougatine onto one of the silicone mats. Cover with the other mat, rolling the nougatine out thinly while it is hot.

- Place the nougatine on baking parchment, then cut it into sixteen discs using the biscuit cutter: press down firmly and turn the cutter to make a clean cut (1). Place the still-warm nougatine discs in the half-sphere mould and press into a rounded shape (2). Leave to cool at room temperature.

PRUNE CREAM

- Cut the prunes into small pieces. In a bowl, whisk together the pectin and sugar.

- Pour the water into a saucepan, add the pectin and sugar and stir to dissolve the sugar. Add the honey and bring to the boil. Add the prunes, lemon zest and vanilla seeds.

- Pour the prune mixture into the food processor and process until smooth. Over a saucepan, press the cream through a drum sieve to make it smooth, then stir with a silicone spatula over a medium heat for 5 to 10 minutes to dry it a little and thicken the prune cream (3).

- Remove the saucepan from the heat and allow the cream to cool before filling the piping bag. Cut the walnuts in half.

- Pipe balls of prune cream into the cooled nougatine half-spheres (4), then place ½ a walnut kernel on top of each ball of cream, pressing down with your finger (5). Refrigerate for about 5 to 10 minutes.

FINISH

- Temper the dark chocolate (see pp. 45–48). Place the tempered chocolate in a small bowl deep enough to completely submerge the caprices. Place the Rhodoïd® (acetate) sheet next to the bowl of chocolate.

- Using the fork, dip the caprices one by one into the dark chocolate. Tap it on the rim of the bowl to remove any excess chocolate, then place the caprices on the Rhodoïd® (acetate) sheet (6).

- Leave the chocolate to harden at room temperature for about 30 minutes.

- Caprices will keep for up to 20 days in a dry place in an airtight container at room temperature.

CHEF'S TIP

Make sure that the temperature of the chocolate does not fall more than 1°C below the tempering temperature. Keep a bain-marie on hand to warm it up for a few seconds if necessary, and stir the chocolate before using again.

Menhirs

BRITTANY

The word "menhir", meaning "stone" in Breton, alludes to the shape of these chocolates that mimics that of the megalithic monuments found near Carnac, where thousands of menhirs stand. Chocolate menhirs were first created in 1967 by François Cartron, a confectioner who worked near Carnac.

FOR 22 MENHIRS

DIFFICULTY

Preparation time: 1 h • **Refrigeration time:** 24 h

GANACHE

60 g dark couverture chocolate 70% • 120 g milk couverture chocolate • 20 g unsweetened cocoa powder • 20 g cocoa paste • 40 g almond and hazelnut praline • 20 g softened butter • 15 g chopped roasted almonds

FINISH

200 g milk chocolate powder or unsweetened cocoa powder

EQUIPMENT

1 piping bag • 4 x 25 cm long confectionery rulers • 1 x 2 cm wide rose petal biscuit cutter • 1 dipping fork • 1 pastry brush

Menhirs

GANACHE

- Melt the dark and milk chocolate with the cocoa powder and cocoa paste over a bain-marie to 50°C.
- Add the praline (1) and stir until smooth. Stir in the butter and chopped roasted almonds. Transfer the ganache to the piping bag.
- Place 3 confectionery rulers, each 1 cm high, parallel to each other on a baking tray lined with baking parchment, leaving a 2.5 cm space between each ruler, then place 1 ruler perpendicular to the 3 rulers to form a straight edge. Pipe the ganache between the rulers to a height of 1 cm (2).
- Place the tray in the refrigerator for 24 hours, until the ganache has hardened.
- Run the blade of a small knife along the rulers to loosen the ganache, then use the biscuit cutter to cut out the menhirs (3).

FINISH

- Put the milk chocolate powder in a bowl.
- Using the dipping fork, coat each ganache with the powder (4). Tap gently and then remove any excess powder with the brush. When using the brush, be careful not to leave any visible marks on the menhirs.
- Menhirs will keep for up to 10 days in a dry place in an airtight container at room temperature.

①

②

③

④

Tas de sel

BRITTANY

FOR 30 TAS DE SEL

DIFFICULTY

Preparation time: 50 min • **Refrigeration time:** 1 h • **Resting time:** 30 min • **Cooking time:** 15 min

SALTED BUTTER CARAMEL GANACHE
110 g dark couverture chocolate 70% • 90 ml cream • 15 g liquid acacia honey • 0.5 g fine "fleur de sel" sea salt • 40 g sugar • 30 g softened butter

COATING
150 g white couverture chocolate • 5 g white granulated sugar

EQUIPMENT
1 cooking thermometer • 1 piping bag • 1 plain 10 mm Ø nozzle • 1 x 3 cm Ø conical silicone mould with 30 imprints • 1 round dipping fork

SALTED BUTTER CARAMEL GANACHE

- Melt the dark chocolate over a bain-marie to 50°C.
- In a small saucepan, bring the cream, honey and "fleur de sel" to the boil, then keep it warm.
- Pour the sugar into another small saucepan and heat it dry to a light caramel (about 155°C). Carefully stop the caramel cooking by drizzling in the hot flavoured cream in several stages. Mix until smooth, then pour it over the melted dark chocolate.
- Stir with a silicone spatula to form a ganache, then add the butter, mixing until smooth. Transfer to the piping bag fitted with the nozzle.
- Fill the mould and refrigerate for 1 hour until hardened. Turn out onto a baking tray lined with baking parchment.

COATING

- Temper the white chocolate (see pp. 45–48).
- Place a sheet of baking parchment next to the bowl of tempered white chocolate. Make sure the ganaches are cold before dipping.
- Using the dipping fork, dip a ganache cone into the chocolate, tap it on the rim of the bowl to remove any excess, then place the coated ganache on the baking parchment. Sprinkle with a pinch of granulated sugar before the white chocolate hardens. Repeat with all the ganache cones.
- Leave the chocolate at room temperature for 30 minutes to harden.
- Tas de sel will keep for up to 20 days in a dry place in an airtight container.

CHEF'S TIPS

Before unmoulding, brush a very thin layer of tempered dark chocolate (chablonnage) on the base of the tas de sel to keep them firm and make them easier to coat. • Make sure that the temperature of the chocolate does not fall more than 1°C below the tempering temperature. Reheat for a few seconds over a bain-marie if necessary.

Dark chocolate sarments

MÉDOC

The Médoc's vineyards are some of the most famous in the world, and the shape of these chocolates mimics the irregular outline of a sarment – the French word for vine shoots. Here, the delicious, tangy flavour comes from combining chocolate and orange.

FOR 25 SARMENTS

DIFFICULTY
Preparation time: 45 min • **Resting time:** 30 min • **Cooking time:** 15 min

INGREDIENTS
100 g dark couverture chocolate 50% • 10 ml orange flavouring

FINISH
10 g flaked almonds, finely chopped

EQUIPMENT
1 Rhodoïd® (acetate) sheet • 1 cooking thermometer • 1 piping bag • 1 plain 4 mm Ø nozzle

- Preheat the oven to 160°C.
- Use a pencil to draw 25 wavy lines 12 cm long on a sheet of baking parchment. Leave a space of 3 cm between each line. Place the paper upside down on a baking tray, then lay the Rhodoïd® (acetate) sheet on it.
- Place the almonds on a baking tray and roast in the oven for 10 minutes, turning over regularly to ensure they are fully roasted. Leave to cool.
- Temper the dark chocolate (see pp. 45–48). When it reaches 50°C, add the orange flavouring to the melted chocolate.
- Fill the piping bag with the flavoured chocolate. Pipe it onto the Rhodoïd® (acetate) sheet following the lines, making sure you do not press too hard on the piping bag to avoid the sarments from being too thick.
- Sprinkle with chopped roasted almonds and leave to harden for 30 minutes at room temperature.
- To avoid breaking them, use a small spatula to carefully lift the sarments from the Rhodoïd® (acetate) sheet.
- Sarments will keep for up to 20 days in a dry place in an airtight container.

Ardoises

ANGERS

Originally from Angers, the capital of Anjou, this confectionery was created to honour the regional tradition of making beautiful slate (ardoise in French) roofs. Recognisable by their colour and shape, ardoises are now part of the region's culinary heritage.

FOR 30 ARDOISES

DIFFICULTY

Preparation time: 1 h • Refrigeration time: 20 min • Cooking time: 10 min

HAZELNUT AND ALMOND NOUGATINE
60 g whole skinned hazelnuts • 60 g whole blanched almonds • 5 g butter

COOKED SUGAR SYRUP
45 ml water • 125 g sugar • 50 g glucose

COATING
150 g white couverture chocolate • 1 drop blue fat-soluble food colouring • 5 g edible silver glitter powder

EQUIPMENT
1 cooking thermometer • 2 silicone mats • 1 ruler • 1 Rhodoïd® (acetate) sheet + 1 sheet cut into 30 squares of 4 cm each • 1 dipping fork • 1 pastry brush

- Preheat the oven to 110°C. Prepare a baking tray lined with baking parchment to soften the nougatine if necessary.
- Using a large knife, coarsely chop the hazelnuts and almonds and set aside.

COOKED SUGAR SYRUP

- Pour the water and sugar into a saucepan, stir until the sugar dissolves, then add the glucose. Heat to a light caramel colour, about 160°C (barley-coloured sugar) on the cooking thermometer.

HAZELNUT AND ALMOND NOUGATINE

- Remove the saucepan of cooked sugar syrup from the heat and add the chopped hazelnuts and almonds (1). Mix, then add the butter. Using a silicone spatula, stir for a few seconds and pour onto one of the silicone mats. Immediately cover with the other mat, then roll it out (2) to a rectangle measuring about 25 x 15 cm x 4 mm thick.
- Carefully remove the top silicone mat and turn the nougatine over onto a chopping board lined with baking parchment and remove the other mat. Using the ruler, cut 3 cm wide strips, then cut 3 cm squares from these (3). If the nougatine hardens, place it on a hot baking tray in the oven for 5 minutes to warm it enough to cut.
- Leave the nougatine squares to cool for about 15 minutes at room temperature.

COATING

- Temper the white chocolate (see pp. 45–48), adding the blue food colouring at 45°C, and stir with a silicone spatula until the colour is even.
- Place the Rhodoïd® (acetate) sheet next to the bowl of tempered chocolate. Using the dipping fork, dip the hazelnut and almond nougatines into the coloured chocolate one by one, then tap it on the rim of the bowl to remove any excess chocolate (4). Place the ardoises on the Rhodoïd® (acetate) sheet, then put 1 small square of Rhodoïd® (acetate) sheet on each, pressing very lightly.
- Refrigerate the ardoises for about 20 minutes. When the chocolate has hardened, carefully lift off the Rhodoïd® (acetate) squares. The chocolate should be cold and glossy, and hard enough so that no marks can be left on it.
- Use the brush to apply a very fine layer of silver powder.
- Ardoises will keep for up to 15 days in a dry place in an airtight container.

CHEF'S TIP

Make sure that the temperature of the chocolate does not fall more than 1°C below the tempering temperature. Keep a bain-marie on hand to warm it up for a few seconds if necessary, and stir the chocolate before using again.

①

②

③

④

International confectionery

Orange marmalade

EUROPE

FOR 1.1 TO 1.3 KG OF MARMALADE

DIFFICULTY ♢

Preparation time: 30 min • **Resting time:** 3 days • **Cooking time:** 1 h 25 min

INGREDIENT
1.4 kg whole organic oranges

SUGAR SYRUP
1 litre water • 1 kg sugar

COOKING SYRUP
1 litre orange juice • 750 g sugar • Juice of ½ lemon • 3 cinnamon sticks • 40 ml rum

EQUIPMENT
1 cooking thermometer • 1 refractometer (optional) • 5 to 6 sterilised 225 ml jam jars

DAY 1
- Prick the oranges with a fork, then place in a large bowl of water for 3 days, changing the water every morning and evening to remove the bitter taste of the orange peel.

DAY 4
- Cut the oranges in half, cut off the ends and remove the seeds. Thinly slice the oranges (1).

COOKING SYRUP
- Prepare the sugar syrup: bring the water and sugar to the boil. Add the orange slices and poach at a simmer until translucent, about 30 minutes, then remove from the heat.
- Chill a plate in the refrigerator.
- Pour the orange juice and sugar into another saucepan. Stir to dissolve the sugar, then add the lemon juice and cinnamon sticks.
- Using a skimmer, place the orange slices in the orange juice mixture (2).
- Bring to the boil, stirring regularly, then skim.
- Continue cooking the marmalade for about 45 minutes, until the temperature reaches 105°C (or 63° Brix on the refractometer, see p. 306). Remove the cinnamon sticks, then stir in the rum.
- Take a drop of marmalade and put it on the cold plate. Tilt the plate. If the marmalade flows slowly, it is ready to transfer to the jars. If not, continue cooking for a few more minutes and check again.
- When cooked, carefully ladle the marmalade into the sterilised jars (3). Close the jars, turn them upside down and leave for 1 minute lid-side down, then turn them back up again and leave to cool at room temperature.
- Marmalade will keep for 1 year in a dark place at room temperature.

CHEF'S TIP

Save the sugar syrup used to poach the orange slices as it can be used for candying citrus fruit supremes.

Lokums

LEBANON

Made with eastern ingredients such as gum arabic and rose water, the origins of lokum – also known as Turkish delight – go back more than 500 years. In Lebanon, they are sandwiched between two biscuits and enjoyed as a snack, while the Turkish version is firmer. They can also be made with nuts or seeds (sesame or pistachio) and flavoured with orange blossom water instead of rose water.

FOR 35 LOKUMS

DIFFICULTY

Preparation time: 15 min • Resting time: 6 h • Cooking time: 40 min

PREPARE THE FRAME
100 g icing sugar • 100 g cornflour

COOKED SUGAR SYRUP
67 ml water • 225 g sugar

- - -

450 ml water • 112 g cornflour • 5 drops red liquid food colouring • 3 g gum arabic powder • 22 ml rose water

EQUIPMENT
1 x 16 x 16 cm and 2 cm high frame • 1 cooking thermometer

PREPARE THE FRAME

- Mix the icing sugar and cornflour in a bowl. Sift a thick layer of the mixture into the frame placed on a baking tray. Set the rest aside on a plate.

COOKED SUGAR SYRUP

- Pour the water and sugar into a saucepan and stir to dissolve the sugar. Heat until the temperature reaches 117°C (soft ball) on the cooking thermometer, then remove from the heat.

- Put the 450 ml of water and the 112 g of cornflour into another saucepan and heat over a medium heat. Stir until the mixture begins to thicken. Reduce the heat to low and stir vigorously without stopping, then add the cooked sugar syrup in five batches.

- Cook for at least 20 minutes at a simmer, stirring constantly. The mixture should be elastic and almost translucent (1).

- Add the previously mixed colouring, gum arabic and rose water (2). Mix and immediately pour into the prepared frame, spreading it out evenly.

- Leave to stand uncovered at room temperature for at least 6 hours. After this time, sprinkle with a little of the remaining icing sugar and cornflour mixture.

- Run the blade of a knife through the icing sugar and cornflour mixture to coat it, then run the knife around the inside edge of the frame to remove the lokum. Cut the lokum into 2.5 cm strips (3). Then, cut the strips into 2.5 cm squares. Roll the squares in the icing sugar and cornflour mixture to prevent them from sticking to each other.

- Lokums coated in icing sugar and cornflour will keep for about 15 days in a dry place in an airtight container.

Wine gums

UNITED KINGDOM

Wine gums are a jelly confectionery of English origin, first sold in London by Charles Gordon Maynard at the beginning of the 20th century.
These little sweets are soft, colourful and often fruit flavoured, and come in many shapes. Despite their name, wine gums contain no alcohol!

FOR 50 WINE GUMS

DIFFICULTY
Preparation time: 40 min • **Resting time:** 24 h 30 min • **Cooking time:** 15 min

INGREDIENTS
3 drops each flavouring (raspberry, strawberry, lemon, mint) • 3 drops each liquid food colouring (red, pink, yellow and green) • 32 g gelatine leaves 200 Bloom • 6 drops lemon juice

COOKED SUGAR SYRUP
100 ml water • 400 g sugar • 350 g glucose

1 bowl cornflour

COATING
Grapeseed oil or 10 g beeswax + 100 g grapeseed oil

EQUIPMENT
1 cooking thermometer • 4 jugs • 1 half-sphere silicone mould with 65 x 2.5 cm Ø imprints • 1 pastry brush • 1 pair thin latex gloves

Wine gums

DAY 1

- Prepare four bowls, each containing a flavouring and its corresponding food colouring (raspberry flavouring and red food colouring; strawberry flavouring and pink food colouring; lemon flavouring and yellow food colouring; and mint flavouring and green food colouring).
- Soften the gelatine leaves in cold water.

COOKED SUGAR SYRUP

- Pour the water and sugar into a large saucepan, stir to dissolve the sugar, then add the glucose. Heat until the temperature reaches 118–120°C (firm ball) on the cooking thermometer (for firmer wine gums, cook to 120°C).
- Squeeze the gelatine leaves to extract as much water as possible, then add them to the cooked sugar syrup with the lemon juice (1). Carefully pour about 225 g into each bowl containing the flavourings and food colouring (2). Stir gently so as not to introduce any air bubbles.
- Fill 1 jug with each colour, then pour quickly into the mould imprints (3). Leave to cool at room temperature for 24 hours.

DAY 2

- Unmould the wine gums, then roll them in the cornflour to coat so they don't stick to each other.
- Sift and gently brush the sweets to remove any excess cornflour, then add shine. To do this, use a brush dipped in a little oil, or melt the wax over a bain-marie and mix it with the 100 g of oil.
- Put the wine gums in a bowl and add 1 tablespoon of the wax-oil mixture (4) and coat them with gloved hands.
- Wine gums will keep for up to 3 weeks in an airtight container at room temperature.

CHEF'S TIP

You can vary the shape of the moulds and the choice of flavourings and food colourings to suit your taste.

①

②

③

④

Tamarind and coconut
lollipops

SOUTH-EAST ASIA

Tamarind is a pod filled with a pulp containing up to four seeds. Sold in a variety of forms (pods, seeds, paste, purée, sauce and concentrate), it is used in a wide range of Asian recipes. A key ingredient in the region, people are very fond of its singularly sweet and sour taste, which has hints of both citrus and caramel.

FOR 30 LOLLIPOPS

DIFFICULTY

Preparation time: 1 h • **Resting time:** 20 min • **Refrigeration time:** 2 h 30 min • **Cooking time:** 15 min

TAMARIND PASTE
100 g tamarind • 300 ml warm water

BANANA-TAMARIND FRUIT JELLY
125 g banana purée • 25 g sugar • 70 g glucose • 6 g yellow pectin • 150 g sugar

ACID SOLUTION
3 g citric acid crystals • 3 ml water

GELATINE MASS
15 g powdered gelatine (or 7½ gelatine leaves) • 75 ml water

COCONUT MARSHMALLOW WITHOUT EGG WHITES
95 g Trimoline® (inverted sugar) • 210 g sugar • 75 g coconut purée • 10 ml Malibu®

- - -

Desiccated coconut for coating

EQUIPMENT
1 Silikomart® sphere lollipop mould with 67 imprints • 1 cooking thermometer • 1 piston funnel • 30 lollipop sticks • 1 stand mixer

Tamarind and coconut lollipops

TAMARIND PASTE

- Soak the tamarind in water for 20 minutes. Squeeze to dilute the pulp in the water, then strain to remove the seeds and fibres. Weigh 150 g of paste.

BANANA-TAMARIND FRUIT JELLY

- In a saucepan, warm the tamarind paste, banana purée, 25 g of sugar and the glucose. Mix the yellow pectin with the 150 g sugar, sprinkle into the previous mixture and whisk well. Cook to 104 or 105°C on the cooking thermometer.

ACID SOLUTION

- Mix the citric acid crystals and water. Remove the fruit jelly from the heat, add the acid solution and mix with a silicone spatula (1). Pour the fruit jelly into the piston funnel, then fill the imprints (2).
- Leave the fruit jelly to set for around 2 hours in the refrigerator. Push a lollipop stick into the centre of each fruit jelly.

GELATINE MASS

- Whisk the powdered gelatine with the cold water in a bowl (if using gelatine leaves instead of powdered gelatine, make sure they are submerged in the water). Refrigerate for at least 30 minutes.

COCONUT MARSHMALLOW WITHOUT EGG WHITES

- Place the Trimoline® in the bowl of the stand mixer fitted with a whisk attachment.
- In a saucepan, heat the sugar and coconut purée to 114°C. Remove from the heat and add the gelatine mass. Carefully pour the hot liquid into the bowl of the stand mixer, mix well, then add the Malibu®. Whisk at low speed until the mixture is fluffy, glossy and soft. (3).
- Carefully remove the fruit jelly lollipops from the silicone mould and place on a baking tray lined with baking parchment. Place the desiccated coconut in a bowl.
- Dip the fruit jelly candies in the marshmallow. Allow the excess marshmallow to fall (4), then dip the lollipops into the coconut to coat (5).
- Turn upright and insert the tamarind and coconut lollipops in a holder, such as a bowl filled with sugar or in polystyrene (6).
- The lollipops can be stored for up to 1 week at room temperature, upright in a polystyrene holder in an airtight box.

CHEF'S TIP

You can add 10% sugar to tamarind paste to balance its acidity.

Vanilla fudge
and coffee toffee

UNITED KINGDOM

Fudge is a soft caramel the origin of which is uncertain. Some say it was invented in the United States, others in the United Kingdom in the south-west of England (Devon, Dorset and Cornwall). It is available in a whole range of flavours, such as coffee, chocolate, orange, etc.

Toffee dates back to the end of the 18th century and is very popular in English-speaking countries. The final consistency depends on how long the sugar has been cooked: the longer it is heated, the harder the toffee becomes.

VANILLA FUDGE

FOR 75 FUDGES

DIFFICULTY

Preparation time: 30 min • Resting time: 3 h
• Cooking time: 15 min

INGREDIENTS

100 ml water • 250 g sugar
• 175 g sweetened condensed milk • 1 g fine "fleur de sel" sea salt • 1 vanilla pod, split lengthways
• 210 g glucose • 105 g butter

Grapeseed oil for the frames and knife

EQUIPMENT

2 x 15 x 15 cm and 2 cm high frames
• 1 cooking thermometer

COFFEE TOFFEE

FOR 25 TOFFEES

DIFFICULTY

Preparation time: 30 min • Resting time: 3 h
• Cooking time: 20 min

COFFEE-COCOA EMULSION

25 g coffee beans • 150 ml cream • 90 g cocoa mass
• 110 g butter • 25 ml Trablit® coffee extract
• 1 g biocarbonate of soda (optional)

Grapeseed oil for the metal frame and knife

COOKED SUGAR SYRUP

75 ml water • 240 g sugar • 25 g glucose

EQUIPMENT

1 x 16 x 16 cm and 2 cm high stainless steel frame
• 1 silicone mat • 1 cooking thermometer • Cellophane

VANILLA FUDGE

- Place the 2 oiled frames onto a baking tray covered with baking parchment.
- Place the water, sugar, sweetened condensed milk, fine "fleur de sel" sea salt and vanilla pod in a saucepan (1). Bring to the boil stirring continously, then add the glucose (2).
- Cook until the temperature reaches 110°C on the cooking thermometer. Add the butter (3), continue stirring with a silicone spatula until the temperature reaches 117°C. Remove the saucepan from the heat and remove the vanilla pod.
- Carefully pour the mixture into the frames and leave to cool for at least 3 hours at room temperature.
- Oil a large knife and cut 2.5 cm squares.
- Store the vanilla fudge for up to 3 weeks in an airtight container away from moisture and heat.

COFFEE TOFFEE

COFFEE-COCOA EMULSION

- Position the oiled frame on a baking tray covered with the silicone mat.
- Preheat the oven to 160°C. Place the coffee beans on a baking tray and roast for 5 minutes.
- Bring the cream to the boil in a small saucepan, then add the coffee beans. Remove from the heat, cover the pan with a lid and leave to infuse for 15 minutes.
- Melt the cocoa mass and butter over a bain-marie. Strain the coffee infused cream through a sieve and weigh 150 g (4). If there isn't enough, add cream. Pour into a saucepan with the coffee extract and bicarbonate of soda. Bring to the boil, then pour over the cocoa mass and melted butter mixture (5). Whisk to emulsify, cover with cling film and set aside at room temperature.

COOKED SUGAR SYRUP

- Add the water and sugar to a saucepan, stir to dissolve the sugar. Bring to the boil, stirring constantly, then add the glucose. Heat until the temperature reaches 155°C (barley sugar) on the cooking thermometer.
- Stop the cooking process by carefully pouring in the coffee-cocoa emulsion (6), continue stirring with a silicone spatula until the temperature reaches 125°C. Remove from the heat.
- Carefully pour the mixture into the frame and leave to cool for at least 3 hours at room temperature.
- Using a large oiled knife, cut out 3 cm squares. Cut out small squares of cellophane paper and wrap the coffee toffees.
- Store in an airtight container for up to 3 weeks.

Butterscotch

UNITED KINGDOM

Despite containing the word "Scotch", butterscotch was actually created at the beginning of the 19th century in Yorkshire, England.

FOR 80 BUTTERSCOTCH

DIFFICULTY
Preparation time: 20 min • **Resting time:** 2 h • **Cooking time:** 15 min

INGREDIENTS
450 g butter • 450 g sugar • 110 g sugar cane molasses • 8 g fine salt

EQUIPMENT
2 x 20 x 12.5 cm and 1 cm high stainless steel trays • 1 cooking thermometer • Cellophane (optional)

- Line the stainless steel trays with baking parchment.
- Melt the butter in a large saucepan over a low heat. Add the sugar, molasses and salt (1).
- Bring to the boil, stirring with a silicone spatula to dissolve the sugars, then cook until the temperature reaches 125°C on the cooking thermometer (2).
- Carefully pour the butterscotch into the stainless steel trays, filling them to the top (3).
- When the butterscotch has hardened (about 2 hours), remove it from the trays by running a knife around the inside edge, then turn it over onto a board lined with baking parchment. Carefully remove the parchment lining the trays.
- Using a large knife, cut it into 2 x 3 cm rectangles. If you wish, cut out pieces of cellophane and wrap the butterscotch in them.
- Butterscotch will keep for up to 3 weeks in a dry place in an airtight container at room temperature.

①

②

③

Dalgona

SOUTH KOREA

Dalgona, also known as "ppopgi", is a Korean confectionery made from just two ingredients: sugar and bicarbonate of soda. Typically flat and originally made with glucose, dalgona was eaten as a street-food snack. A special mould is used to stamp the design onto the surface. Many kits are available, but you can just as easily use biscuit cutters to create original shapes.

FOR 4 DALGONA

DIFFICULTY

Preparation time: 15 min • Cooking time: 8 min

INGREDIENTS

60 g sugar • 4 pinches bicarbonate of soda • Sugar for the dalgona disc (if using a kit)

EQUIPMENT

1 dalgona kit or 1 x 8 cm Ø round cutter • 1 metal or wooden chopstick • Decorative cutters

NOT SO SIMPLE!

Dalgona is sold whole: it is round, with an indented design in the centre. A popular Korean game involves separating the stamped pattern from the outer part of the sweet without breaking it. It sounds easy, but it can actually be very difficult depending on the shape of the pattern.

Dalgona

METHOD WITH A KIT

- On the work surface, crush a handful of sugar using the dalgona disc. Sprinkle a little into the stainless steel square that comes with the kit.
- Place the 5 to 7 cm diameter mini copper pan over a medium heat. Pour in 15 g of sugar and stir with a chopstick until the caramel is light amber in colour (1).
- Add a pinch of bicarbonate of soda (2) and stir briskly until the sugar is frothy (3).
- Quickly pour it into the stainless steel square (4). Wait 4 or 5 seconds, then gently press the dalgona disc – previously dipped in the crushed sugar – for 3 or 4 seconds (5).
- Remove the disc and immediately mark the dalgona with the cutter of your choice (6). Repeat the operation three times, using a different cutter for each dalgona.
- Leave to cool and enjoy immediately.

METHOD WITHOUT A KIT

- Use the cutter and a felt-tip pen to draw four 8 cm diameter discs on a sheet of baking parchment. Turn the sheet over and place it on a baking tray.
- Melt all the sugar in a small 10 to 15 cm diameter frying pan over a medium heat, then caramelise to a light amber caramel, stirring with a chopstick. Add the bicarbonate of soda and stir briskly until the caramel is frothy.
- Quickly pour four small discs about 8 cm in diameter onto the marked baking tray. Cut out immediately with the round cutter, then use decorative biscuit cutters to make a pattern on the surface in the centre of each dalgona.
- Leave to cool and enjoy immediately.

CHEF'S TIP

Dip the caramel-coated chopstick in the bicarbonate of soda two or three times as this will ensure you don't use too much.

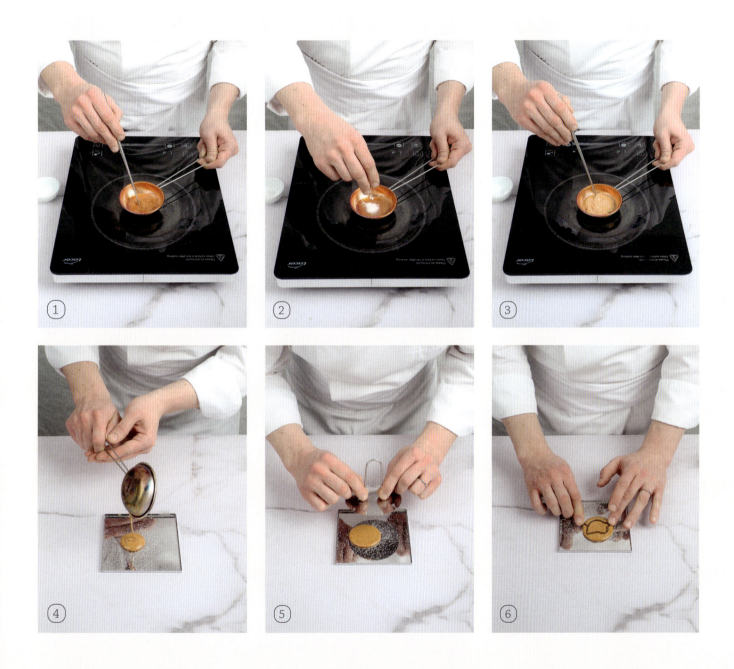

Chikki

INDIA

This traditional Indian confectionery is most often made with peanuts, but can also be made with chickpeas, sesame seeds, puffed rice, dried coconut, almonds or pistachios. Ghee is a kind of clarified butter and a very important ingredient in Indian cuisine.

FOR 1 KG OF CHIKKI

DIFFICULTY

Preparation time: 20 min • Resting time: 3 h • Cooking time: 25 min

INGREDIENTS

500 g skinless peanuts • 550 g muscovado sugar • 20 g ghee (or clarified butter) • 25 ml water

Grapeseed oil for the baking tray

EQUIPMENT

1 cooking thermometer

- Preheat the oven to 170°C. Place the peanuts on a baking tray and roast for 15 to 18 minutes, depending on how dark you want them. After taking them out of the oven, lightly chop the peanuts and set them aside.
- Preheat a large non-stick frying pan over a low heat. Add the sugar, ghee and water and stir until the sugar has melted. Heat it slowly, stirring constantly, until the mixture reaches soft crack stage (or the temperature reaches 130°C on the cooking thermometer, making sure it does not touch the bottom of the pan). Drop a few drops of cooked sugar into a bowl of cold water. The sugar should harden immediately and become brittle.
- Add the roasted peanuts and stir until they are coated with the cooked sugar. Remove the pan from the heat and carefully pour the mixture onto an oiled baking tray. Using a metal spoon or oiled spatula, flatten the chikki to an even thickness.
- When the chikki is almost cool, use a large knife to cut it into rectangles to the desired size. Leave to cool for 3 hours at room temperature.
- Chikki will keep for up to 1 week in a cool dry place in an airtight container.

CHEF'S TIP

Other unrefined sugars can be used instead of muscovado sugar.
Results may vary depending on the kind of sugar used as some are drier than others.

Stuffed dates

MEDITERRANEAN

FOR 12 STUFFED DATES

DIFFICULTY
Preparation time: 25 min

INGREDIENTS
12 large dried dates • 260 g almond paste (see p. 42) • 3 to 5 ml flavouring of your choice (orange blossom water or rose water, for example) • 1 drop pistachio green liquid food colouring • 1 drop red liquid food colouring • 3 walnut kernels

EQUIPMENT
1 pair thin latex gloves

- Prepare the almond paste.
- Make an incision halfway through the dates and remove the stones.
- Place the almond paste on the work surface, make a small well in the centre, add the flavouring and fold the paste over it. Gently knead until the flavouring is well incorporated.
- Divide the almond paste into three 85 g pieces. Set aside one third, which will not be coloured. Place the other two on baking parchment and press down a little to form a small well in the centre. Add the pistachio green food colouring to one well and the red food colouring to the other. Wearing gloves, work the colouring into the almond paste until one is an even pale green and the other is pink.
- Shape each of the three amounts into 1 cm thick ropes, then cut them to the same length as the dates.
- Stuff 3 dates with the plain stuffing, 3 dates with the green stuffing and 3 dates with the pink stuffing. Place a walnut kernel on top of the 3 dates filled with the plain almond paste.
- Roll out the remaining plain, pink and green stuffings separately to a thickness of 0.5 cm. Make 3 two-colour twists, then 1 three-colour plait. Cut to the length of the remaining 4 dates. Stuff each one with a length of twisted or plaited almond paste.
- Stuffed dates will keep for at least 1 month in an airtight container at room temperature.

CHEF'S TIPS

Choose good quality dates as they are less sweet and tend to be fleshier.
• Feel free to top the dates with other nuts to decorate.

TURRÓN

HALVA

Turrón

SPAIN

Turrón is the most popular confectionery product in Spain. The two main artisanal varieties are the hard-textured Alicante turrón and the soft-textured Jijona turrón, which contains ground almonds instead of whole ones.

FOR 16 BARS OF TURRÓN

DIFFICULTY

Preparation time: 45 min • **Resting time:** 1 h • **Cooking time:** 25 min

INGREDIENTS

500 g whole blanched almonds • 2 wafer sheets

Grapeseed oil for the frame

MERINGUE
35 g egg whites • 18 g sugar

COOKED SUGAR SYRUP
70 ml water • 200 g sugar • 100 g glucose

- - -

250 g honey

EQUIPMENT

1 x 16 x 16 cm and 2 cm high stainless steel frame • 1 stand mixer • 1 cooking thermometer • 1 chef's blowtorch

- Preheat the oven to 170°C. Place the almonds on a baking tray and roast for 10 minutes, then keep warm.
- Cut the wafer sheets into two 16 x 16 cm squares. Place the oiled frame on a sheet of baking parchment on a baking tray, then place a square of wafer sheet in the bottom.

MERINGUE

- In the bowl of the stand mixer, whisk the egg white until frothy, then increase the speed and continue until stiff peaks form. Whisk in the sugar to stiffen the meringue.

COOKED SUGAR SYRUP

- Pour the water and sugar into a saucepan, stir until the sugar dissolves, then add the glucose. Heat until the temperature reaches 145°C (hard crack) on the cooking thermometer, while continuing to whisk the meringue mixture. Carefully drizzle it over the meringue and continue whisking until fully incorporated.

- Meanwhile, heat the honey in another saucepan until the temperature reaches 130°C on the cooking thermometer. Slowly drizzle it into the previous mixture, whisking it in gently. Increase the speed and whisk for about 3 minutes or until firm.
- Replace the whisk with a paddle attachment and continue mixing at a slow speed. Using the blowtorch, heat the sides of the bowl, leaving the machine running for about 4 to 5 minutes or until you have a firm, paste-like consistency.
- Add the hot almonds and fold them in with a spatula.
- Pour the turrón into the frame, cover with baking parchment and smooth with a rolling pin. Remove the parchment and place the other square of wafer sheet on top, rolling with the rolling pin to ensure it adheres. Leave to cool at room temperature for at least 1 hour before cutting the turrón into 16 cm x 1 cm bars.
- Turrón will keep for up to 4 weeks in a dry place in an airtight container.

Halva

LEBANON

Made with just three ingredients, halva was adopted by many countries in the Middle East, South Asia and Europe as their own special confectionery. But halva, halavah or aluva is actually Persian and means "sweetness and sugar". In Lebanon, it is served on flat bread with fruit and honey.

FOR 14 HALVA

DIFFICULTY

Preparation time: 10 min • Refrigeration time: 12 h • Cooking time: 10 min

INGREDIENTS

75 g blanched pistachios • 200 g icing sugar • 150 g milk powder • 280 g tahini (sesame paste)

EQUIPMENT

1 x 14 x 14 cm and 4.5 cm high frame

- Line the inside of the frame with cling film and place on a baking tray, leaving about 5 cm of extra cling film around the edges to make it easier to unmould.
- Preheat the oven to 170°C.
- Coarsely chop the pistachios, place on a baking tray and roast for 10 minutes. Leave to cool and sprinkle over the bottom of the frame (they will be on top when the halva is finished and turned over).
- Sift the icing sugar into a bowl, then add the milk powder and tahini. Using a spatula, stir until crumbly and slightly powdery. Fill the frame with the mixture to a height of about 4 cm, then press the entire surface with your hand to pack the halva mixture into the frame as tightly as possible. Smooth the surface with a spatula.
- Fold the extra cling film over the top and refrigerate for at least 12 hours.
- Unmould, remove the cling film and cut in half lengthways, then cut each half into bars about 2 cm wide.
- Store at room temperature for up to 3 to 4 weeks.

CHEF'S TIPS

You can add a small amount of the pistachios to the halva mixture • You can use other nuts instead of pistachios if you wish • Make sure you use a good quality tahini (sesame paste).

Cremino

ITALY

This confectionery consists of two layers of hazelnut chocolate with a lighter coloured flavoured chocolate in the middle. Invented in the second half of the 19th century by Ferdinando Baratti, cremino was sold in Baratti & Milano, the shop he and his partner, Edoardo Milano, owned in Turin.

FOR 100 CREMINOS

DIFFICULTY

Preparation time: 45 min • **Refrigeration time:** 1 h 30 min

INGREDIENTS

200 g milk couverture chocolate • 110 g hazelnut paste • 125 g white couverture chocolate • 130 g pistachio paste

DECORATION

Gold leaf (optional)

EQUIPMENT

1 x 20 x 20 cm stainless steel frame • 1 Rhodoïd® (acetate) sheet • 1 cooking thermometer

Cremino

- Place the frame on the Rhodoïd® (acetate) sheet.
- Melt the milk chocolate over a bain-marie to 45°C. Remove the bowl from the bain-marie, then add the hazelnut paste, mixing with a silicone spatula until smooth.
- Melt the white chocolate over a bain-marie to 45°C. Remove the bowl from the bain-marie, then add the pistachio paste, mixing with a silicone spatula until smooth (1).
- Pour half of the milk chocolate-hazelnut mixture into the frame (approximately 155 g) (2). Gently shake the Rhodoïd® (acetate) sheet to smooth the surface, then leave to harden in the refrigerator for 30 minutes. Set the bowl with the other half of the milk chocolate-hazelnut mixture aside at room temperature.
- Pour the white chocolate-pistachio mixture into the frame on top of the first layer (3) and leave to harden in the refrigerator for 30 minutes.
- If the reserved milk chocolate-hazelnut mixture has hardened, heat the bowl a little over a bain-marie until melted, but do not heat it to more than 30°C. Pour it into the frame, making sure the layer is level.
- Leave to harden in the refrigerator for 30 minutes, then turn the frame over and carefully unmould onto a chopping board.
- Dip the blade of a large knife in hot water, wipe the blade dry. Cut it into 2 cm wide strips and then into squares (4).
- Cremino will keep in an airtight container in the refrigerator for up to 3 or 4 weeks.

CHEF'S TIP

You can also spread a very thin layer of tempered dark chocolate (chablonnage) on one side of the cremino before cutting it as this will serve as a base and help to keep them firm.

Gianduja
and gianduiotto

ITALY

The story goes that gianduja was the result of a blockade imposed by Napoleon in 1806. This made cocoa hard to come by, not to mention very expensive. Chocolate makers in Piedmont began making chocolate by replacing part of the cocoa mass with hazelnuts. However, the real craze for this chocolate started during Carnival celebrations in Turin in 1865, when gianduja was handed out by masked characters.

The traditional way of making gianduiotto is to use spatulas to shape tempered chocolate into ingots, which are then wrapped in foil. A simpler way of making them is by pouring the chocolate into a mould of the same shape. Given its melt-in-the-mouth texture, it is rarely sold when the weather gets warm.

FOR 450 G OF GIANDUJA OR 24 GIANDUIOTTO

DIFFICULTY

Preparation time: 1 h • **Refrigeration time:** 45 min • **Cooking time:** 10 min

INGREDIENTS

150 g whole hazelnuts • 150 g icing sugar • 150 g milk couverture chocolate

EQUIPMENT

1 food processor • 1 Silikomart® gianduiotto silicone mould with 24 imprints • 1 cooking thermometer • 1 piping bag

Gianduja and gianduiotto

GIANDUJA

- Preheat the oven to 170°C. Place the hazelnuts on a baking tray and roast for 10 minutes. Once out of the oven, place the hazelnuts in a clean cloth and rub them together to remove the skins. Leave to cool.
- Put the cooled hazelnuts and icing sugar in the bowl of a food processor (1). Grind until smooth.
- Melt the milk chocolate over a bain-marie to 40°C, then pour it over the mixture in the food processor (2). Blend until smooth.
- Gianduja will keep for up to 4 weeks in an airtight container at room temperature or used to make gianduiotto.

GIANDUIOTTO

- Place the silicone mould on a baking tray lined with baking parchment.
- Temper the gianduja to 29°C, as for milk chocolate (see p. 45). Transfer to the piping bag, then fill the mould imprints (3). Tap the baking tray to smooth the surface of the gianduiotto.
- Leave in the refrigerator for 45 minutes, or set aside in a cool place (16°C) overnight.
- Gently unmould the gianduiotto (4).
- Gianduiotto will keep in an airtight container in the refrigerator for up to 4 weeks.

①

②

③

④

Mozartkugel

AUSTRIA

Created in Salzburg in 1890 by Paul Fürst, Mozartkugel are part of Austria's culinary heritage. Its name comes from the famous composer Mozart, who hailed from this town, and from its shape, "kugel", which is German for "ball".

FOR 50 MOZARTKUGEL

DIFFICULTY

Preparation time: 1 h • Refrigeration time: 30 min

PISTACHIO MARZIPAN

½ recipe for almond paste (see p. 42), replacing the almonds with blanched pistachios

ALMOND PASTE

495 g almond paste (see p. 42) • 5 ml kirsch • 15 g unsweetened cocoa powder

COATING

300 g dark couverture chocolate 70%

EQUIPMENT

3 soft acetate guitar sheets • 1 cooking thermometer • 1 round dipping fork

Mozartkugel

PISTACHIO MARZIPAN

- When the pistachio marzipan has cooled and rested, shape it into a rope.

ALMOND PASTE

- Prepare the almond paste.
- For the plain almond paste: take 345 g of almond paste and shape it into a rope.
- For the cocoa almond paste: place the remaining almond paste on the work surface. Make a well in the centre and add the kirsch and sifted cocoa. Smear the paste by pushing away from you with the palm of your hand (fraser) until smooth, then shape it into a short rope (1).

ASSEMBLY

- Shape the plain almond paste into a thin rope cut into 9 g pieces (2) then roll into balls. Do the same with the cocoa almond paste, cutting it into 7 g pieces.
- Place the balls of cocoa almond paste between two soft acetate guitar sheets, then flatten them into discs 5 cm in diameter using a rolling pin. Flatten the balls of plain almond paste into discs 6 cm in diameter (3).
- Cut the pistachio marzipan into 5 g pieces, then roll into balls (3).
- Place a ball of pistachio marzipan on a disc of cocoa almond paste, then wrap it around the pistachio centre and shape into a ball (4).
- Repeat the operation, enclosing the ball of cocoa almond paste in a disc of plain almond paste (5).
- Leave the balls covered in cling film in the refrigerator for 30 minutes.

COATING

- Temper the dark chocolate (see pp. 45–48). Using the fork, dip the balls into the chocolate (6). Shake gently to remove any excess, then place them on the soft acetate guitar sheet. If you wish, as soon as the chocolate starts to harden, roll each ball on the soft acetate guitar sheet to form little peaks all over the surface. Leave the chocolate to harden for 10 to 15 minutes at room temperature.
- Mozartkugel will keep for up to 4 weeks in a dry place in an airtight container at room temperature.

CHEF'S TIP

Make sure that the temperature of the chocolate does not fall more than 1°C below the tempering temperature. Keep a bain-marie on hand to warm it up for a few seconds if necessary, and stir the chocolate before using again.

Schokoküss

GERMANY

The German word schokoküss, first mentioned in 1829, translates as "chocolate kiss" in English. The traditional recipe used a type of meringue made from egg whites and sugar instead of marshmallow. Variations can be found around the world, including tea cakes in the UK and floedeboller in Denmark.

FOR 25 TO 30 SCHOKOKÜSS

DIFFICULTY

Preparation time: 1 h 30 min • **Refrigeration time:** 2 h • **Freezing time:** 1 h • **Cooking time:** 15 min

WAFERS

50 g softened butter • 100 g icing sugar • 1 pinch salt • 1 g vanilla powder • 62 g flour • 75 g egg whites

GELATINE MASS

19 g powdered gelatine 200 Bloom (or 9½ gold gelatine leaves) • 95 ml water

MARSHMALLOW

65 g egg whites • 120 ml water • 395 g sugar • 50 g glucose • 1 g vanilla powder

COATING

300 g dark couverture chocolate 70%

EQUIPMENT

3 piping bags • 1 waffle iron or 1 small frying pan • 1 x 4 cm Ø biscuit cutter • 1 wire rack • 1 stand mixer • 1 cooking thermometer • 1 plain 12 mm Ø nozzle

Schokoküss

WAFERS

- In a bowl, mix the butter, icing sugar, salt and vanilla. Gradually add the flour and egg whites. Beat until smooth. Fill 1 piping bag with the wafer batter and leave it to rest in the refrigerator for 1 hour.
- Pipe small mounds of batter about 6 cm in diameter on the waffle iron (or small frying pan) and cook. Place the baked wafers on baking parchment and cut out discs using the biscuit cutter (1). Leave to cool on the rack.

GELATINE MASS

- Whisk the powdered gelatine with the cold water in a bowl (if using gelatine leaves instead of powdered gelatine, make sure they are submerged in the water). Refrigerate for at least 30 minutes.

MARSHMALLOW

- Whisk the egg whites to soft peaks in the bowl of the stand mixer fitted with a whisk attachment.
- Pour the water and sugar into a saucepan, stir to dissolve the sugar, then add the glucose and cook until the temperature reaches 130°C (soft crack) on the cooking thermometer. Remove from the heat and add the gelatine mass.
- Carefully drizzle over the egg whites while whisking on a slow speed, then increase the speed and whisk briskly for 5 minutes, or until the mixture thickens but is still supple. The marshmallow should be about 30°C.
- Fill 1 piping bag fitted with the nozzle, then pipe nice round balls onto the wafers, making sure they are spaced well apart on the rack (2). Freeze for at least 1 hour.

COATING

- Place the rack over a rimmed dish.
- Temper the dark chocolate (see pp. 45–48). Transfer the tempered dark chocolate to 1 piping bag, cut off the end, then pipe directly over the balls, allowing the chocolate to coat the still frozen marshmallow (3).
- Leave the chocolate to harden a little, then, using a spatula, carefully lift the schokokuss from the rack and place on a baking tray lined with baking parchment (4).
- Refrigerate the schokokuss for about 30 minutes to allow the chocolate to harden.
- Schokoküss can be stored for up to 1 week in a dry place in an airtight container at room temperature.

Brigadeiro

BRAZIL

With a melt-in-the-mouth centre and crunchy outer layer, brigadeiro are one of Brazil's most popular sweets. Created in the 1940s during the war, at a time when access to ingredients was limited, they are made with just a few easy-to-find ingredients that can be stored in the pantry.

FOR 24 BRIGADEIRO

DIFFICULTY

Preparation time: 20 min • Refrigeration time: 2 h • Cooking time: 20 to 25 min

INGREDIENTS

150 ml milk • 20 g chocolate powder (or unsweetened cocoa powder) • 395 g sweetened condensed milk • 15 g butter + extra for the baking tray

---

Chocolate vermicelli for coating

EQUIPMENT

1 pastry brush • 1 pair thin latex gloves

- Brush the baking tray with butter and set aside.
- Pour the milk and chocolate powder into a small saucepan. Stir over a low heat until the chocolate has completely melted.
- Add the sweetened condensed milk and butter. Bring to the boil and cook for 15 to 20 minutes, stirring constantly with a silicone spatula, until the mixture thickens.
- Remove the saucepan from the heat and pour the mixture into the buttered baking tray. Leave to cool for about 2 hours in the refrigerator.
- Put the chocolate vermicelli in a shallow dish. Wearing gloves, scoop out a spoonful of the brigadeiro mixture and shape into balls 2.5 cm in diameter. Roll them in the vermicelli to coat well.
- Brigadeiro will keep for up to 5 days in an airtight container in the refrigerator.

Modern confectionery

Pressed fruit bars

These bars are very easy to prepare for a healthy, tasty and filling snack. They are perfect for breakfast or for an energy boost. In addition to dried fruit, they contain rolled oats rich in protein, vitamins and minerals, which are very popular in Anglo-Saxon countries.

FOR 12 PRESSED FRUIT BARS

DIFFICULTY
Preparation time: 30 min • **Drying time:** 1 h • **Refrigeration time:** 30 min

INGREDIENTS
295 g dried pitted dates • 30 g dried apricots • 30 g dried cranberries • 35 g rolled oats • 40 g hazelnuts • 15 g dried raspberries (see p. 246) • 65 g pecan nuts

EQUIPMENT
2 x 25 cm long confectionery rulers • 1 food processor

- Set the confectionery rulers, 1 cm high and 12 cm apart on a sheet of baking parchment.
- Place the dates, apricots and cranberries in the bowl of a food processor. Blend until a paste forms. Add the rolled oats, hazelnuts, raspberries and pecan nuts. Blend until well combined.
- Pour the preparation between the confectionery rulers, then cover with baking parchment. Using a rolling pin, roll out to form a rectangle of about 12 x 18 cm and 1 cm high.
- Leave to dry for about 1 hour at room temperature or refrigerate for about 30 minutes.
- Using a large knife, cut into 12 x 6 x 3 cm bars. The bars will remain a little soft.
- Store the pressed fruit bars for up to 3 weeks in an airtight container at room temperature, away from humidity.

PEARS CANDIED IN BIRCH SUGAR

REDUCED SUGAR RASPBERRY JAM

Pears candied
in birch sugar

Birch sugar, or xylitol, is a natural sweetener that comes from the tree of the same name. It is a good substitute for white sugar as it is low in calories and has a very low glycaemic index. It is also non-acidifying.

FOR 1.5 KG OF CANDIED PEARS

DIFFICULTY ◯◯◯

Preparation time: 1 h • Resting time: 8 days • Cooking time: 40 min

INGREDIENTS
1.5 kg ripe Curé pears (mini), still firm • ½ tsp salt

ACIDULATED WATER
2 litres cold water • Juice of 1 lemon

SYRUP
1.5 litres water • 600 g birch sugar (xylitol) • 425 g glucose • Glucose for day 8

EQUIPMENT
1 refractometer

DAY 1

- Peel the pears, they should be whole but with the stems left on. As you peel them, put them into the acidulated water (made by mixing the water with the lemon juice) until all the fruit has been prepared. Drain the pears, put them into a saucepan of cold salted water, bring to the boil and simmer for 20 minutes. The pears should be slightly soft.

- Prepare the syrup according to the recipe on p. 36, then allow it to cool to 80°C (no higher, as syrup that is too hot will make the pears impermeable) and pour it over the pears.

DAYS 2 TO 8

- Every day, boil the sugar syrup for about 2 minutes to reach the Brix density indicated (see pp. 36–37). Allow the syrup to cool to 80°C before pouring over the pears. On day 8, add the glucose to the syrup (10% of its weight, see p. 37) before boiling.

- Pears candied in birch sugar will keep in a dark place in an airtight container at room temperature for 1 year.

CHEF'S TIPS

Pears to be candied must be at the peak of ripeness; if they are too ripe, they will fall apart during the candying process. On the other hand, if the fruit is too firm and not ripe enough, the syrup will not saturate it properly. • Pears can be candied for 10 to 15 days. To do this, make sure that the syrup is not too dense and does not exceed 70° Brix.

Reduced sugar
raspberry jam

Maltitol is made from maize or barley and is produced by hydrogenating maltose. Used as a sugar substitute and stabiliser, it has fewer calories than sugar and a low glycaemic index. Similar in taste to sugar, maltitol has the same sweetening power as sugar. It is also heat-resistant, making it ideal for substituting sugar in jams.

FOR 500 G OF RASPBERRY JAM

DIFFICULTY
Preparation time: 20 min • **Maceration time:** 3 or 4 h • **Cooking time:** 1 h

INGREDIENTS
350 g maltitol • 200 g sugar • 8 g NH pectin • 20 ml lemon juice • 1 kg raspberries • 1 star anise broken into 5 pieces

EQUIPMENT
1 muslin cloth • 1 cooking thermometer (or 1 refractometer) • 2 sterilised 250 ml jam jars

- Put the maltitol, sugar, pectin, lemon juice and raspberries in a saucepan. Cover and leave to macerate for 3 or 4 hours.
- Chill a plate in the refrigerator.
- Add the star anise pieces wrapped in the muslin and heat over a medium heat. When it comes to the boil, skim to remove any foam and impurities from the surface.
- Continue cooking until the temperature reaches 105°C on the cooking thermometer (or 63° Brix on a refractometer, see p. 306).
- Take a drop of jam and put it on the cold plate. Tilt the plate. If the jam flows slowly, it is ready to transfer to the jars. If not, continue cooking for a few minutes and check again.
- When cooked, remove the muslin and carefully ladle the jam into the sterilised jars. Close the jars, turn them upside down and leave for 1 minute lid-side down, then turn them back up again and leave to cool at room temperature.
- Raspberry jam will keep for 2 to 3 months in a dark place at room temperature.

Fruit crisps
and dried fruit

Available in a variety of colours and shapes, fruit crisps and dried fruit are not only delicious, but can also be used as a table decoration, or broken up and used in recipes to enhance flavours. We love their great texture and vibrant flavours.

FRUIT CRISPS

FOR 1 BOWL OF FRUIT

DIFFICULTY

Preparation time: 30 min • Drying time: 6 to 12 h
• Cooking time: 10 min

SUGAR SYRUP
250 ml water • 125 g birch sugar (xylitol)
• Juice of 1 lemon

CHOICE OF FRUIT
1 small pineapple • 1 organic orange
• 1 small organic apple • 1 small organic pear
• 1 organic kiwi • 3 kumquats

EQUIPMENT
2 silicone mats • 1 dehydrator (optional)

DRIED FRUIT

FOR ½ PUNNET OF FRUIT

DIFFICULTY

Preparation time: 5 min • Drying time: 10 to 12 h

INGREDIENT
1 punnet organic raspberries or strawberries

EQUIPMENT
1 dehydrator

CHEF'S TIPS

The syrup in which the fruit was poached can be saved and reused for other fruits.
• Dehydrate small fruit in syrup, such as kiwi or kumquat, for between 4 and 12 hours, any longer than this, they may become bitter. Depending on their size and the amount of water they contain, pineapples and oranges will take longer.

FRUIT CRISPS

SUGAR SYRUP

- Pour the water and sugar into a clean, dry saucepan, stir to dissolve the sugar, then bring to the boil and add the lemon juice.
- Wash the fruit. Peel the pineapple, but leave the skin on the other fruit. Cut into very thin slices (1) then place in the simmering sugar syrup (2). Leave to cook for about 10 minutes, until the fruit slices are translucent.

OVEN METHOD

- Preheat the oven to 40°C.
- Drain the fruit slices from the sugar syrup (3) and place them on the silicone mats, leaving a little space between each slice (4). Leave in the oven for at least 6 hours.

DEHYDRATOR METHOD

- Place the fruit drained from the syrup on dehydrator racks or trays and place in the dehydrator. Dry overnight at 50°C.
- Fruit crisps will keep for up to 3 weeks in a dry place in a large airtight container, preferably with a sheet of baking parchment between each layer.

DRIED FRUIT

- Put the raspberries (or strawberries) on a rack or tray with a space in between them in the dehydrator and dry for 10 to 12 hours at 50°C. Dehydrated raspberries can be stored whole or broken up and added to mixtures, such as marshmallows (see p. 70), or pressed fruit bars (see p. 240).
- Dried fruit without sugar syrup will keep for up to 1 to 2 months in a dry place in an airtight container.

①

②

③

④

Granola bars

Granola is a mixture of cereals, particularly oats, and dried fruit, which are oven-roasted with natural fats and sugar. The cocoa butter used is neutral in flavour and acts as a binding agent in this recipe, so that the granola can fully express its flavour.

FOR 6 GRANOLA BARS

DIFFICULTY

Preparation time: 1 h • **Resting time:** 30 min • **Cooking time:** 30 min

INGREDIENTS

10 g whole hazelnuts • 10 g whole almonds • 10 g whole pecan nuts • 10 g whole pistachio nuts • 40 g rolled oats • 10 g golden linseeds (flax seeds) • 30 g dried cranberries • 30 g dried apricots • 10 g dried pitted dates • 25 g cocoa butter • 5 ml olive oil • 40 g honey

COATING

150 g dark couverture chocolate 70%

Grapeseed oil for the moulds

EQUIPMENT

6 x 3.5 x 11 cm rectangular stainless steel moulds

Granola bars

GRANOLA

- Lightly oil the stainless steel moulds, then place on a baking tray lined with baking parchment.
- Finely chop the hazelnuts, almonds, pecan nuts and pistachios, then place in a bowl. Add the rolled oats and linseed and mix.
- Add the diced cranberries, apricots and dates and mix (1).
- Warm the cocoa butter, pour over the nuts, fruit and seed mixture along with the olive oil and mix well (2).
- In a small saucepan, bring the honey to the boil over high heat. Pour into the bowl and stir to coat the nuts, fruits and seeds.
- Preheat the oven to 180°C. Spoon about 35 g of granola into each mould (3), then, using a small bent spatula, press the granola down well (4). Bake in the oven for 10 minutes, then lower the temperature to 160°C and continue baking for around 15 minutes, until the granola is golden brown.
- Remove from the oven and wait a few minutes before carefully removing the moulds from the hot granola bars (5). Leave the bars to cool on the baking tray.

COATING

- Temper the dark chocolate (see pp. 45–48).
- Coarsely chop the chocolate, heat two thirds over a bain-marie until the temperature reaches 45–50°C. Remove from the bain-marie and add the remaining chopped chocolate. Mix until the added chocolate melts and cools the entire batch to between 30 and 32°C. Test to see if the chocolate is well tempered and ready to use.
- Dip the bases of each bar in the tempered chocolate (6). Place on baking parchment and leave the chocolate to harden at room temperature for 30 minutes.
- Store the granola bars for up to 2 weeks in an airtight container at room temperature, away from humidity.

CHEF'S TIPS

For a vegan alternative, replace the honey with unheated maple syrup.
- Other fruits, such as raisins, can be used instead of apricots.

Reduced sugar
pecan praline

Pecan nuts, the fruit of the pecan tree, are native to the United States and Mexico. Sweeter than other nuts, they are a popular ingredient in many recipes, including this praline.

FOR 250 G OF PECAN PRALINE

DIFFICULTY
Preparation time: 40 min • Cooking time: 15 min

INGREDIENTS
150 g unrefined cane sugar • 50 g isomalt • 250 g pecan nuts • ½ dried vanilla pod • 2 g fine "fleur de sel" sea salt

EQUIPMENT
1 silicone mat • 1 food processor • 1 sterilised 250 ml jam jar

- Place the silicone mat on a baking tray.
- In a saucepan, heat the unrefined cane sugar and isomalt dry without stirring until a light caramel forms (170°C).
- Add the pecan nuts and continue cooking until the caramel turns brown. Pour the pecan caramel onto the silicone mat and leave at room temperature to cool completely.
- Break the pecan caramel into small pieces and put them in a food processor. Add the vanilla and fine "fleur de sel" sea salt. Process the caramel, stopping regularly to clean the sides of the bowl, until the mixture is smooth and even.
- Transfer the praline to the sterilised jar and store in a dark place at room temperature for up to 2 months.

USING ISOMALT

Although it falls into the sugar-alcohol category, isomalt has very little in common with alcohol, aside from basic structural chemical similarities. When sold commercially, isomalt is an opaque white granule, similar in size to sugar, but has completely different characteristics. Half as sweet as sucrose, it is used in baked goods and confectionery where less sweetness and fewer calories are required. Absorbed by the body only to a limited degree, there are, however, advantages to using isomalt when compared with other ingredients. Be careful: use it in moderation.

Soft nougat
with aquafaba

FOR 40 SOFT NOUGATS WITH AQUAFABA

DIFFICULTY ◠◠

Preparation time: 45 min • Drying time: 12 h • Cooking time: 25 min

INGREDIENTS
160 g whole almonds • 2 wafer sheets • 80 g cocoa butter • 60 g blanched pistachios • 30 g dried cranberries • 30 g dried apricots

AQUAFABA MERINGUE
90 g aquafaba (see p. 27) • 22 g unrefined cane sugar

COOKED SUGAR SYRUP
140 ml water • 200 g sugar • 100 g trehalose • 100 g isomalt • 140 g glucose

- - -

250 g honey

EQUIPMENT
2 silicone mats • 1 stand mixer • 1 cooking thermometer • 1 chef's blowtorch

---

- Preheat the oven to 170°C. Place the almonds on a baking tray and roast for 10 minutes, then leave to cool. Set aside.
- Place 1 wafer sheet on a silicone mat.

AQUAFABA MERINGUE
- Pour the aquafaba into the bowl of the stand mixer and whisk until frothy. Add the unrefined cane sugar and whisk until a stiff meringue clings to the tip of the whisk.

COOKED SUGAR SYRUP
- Pour the water, sugar, trehalose and isomalt into a saucepan, stir to dissolve the sugars, then add the glucose and heat to 155°C (barley-coloured sugar) on the cooking thermometer. Carefully drizzle over the aquafaba meringue while continuing to whisk the aquafaba meringue mixture at medium speed.
- Meanwhile, heat the honey in another saucepan until the temperature reaches 130°C on the cooking thermometer. Slowly drizzle it into the previous mixture and whisk gently.
- Replace the whisk with a paddle attachment and mix on a slow speed. Using the blowtorch, heat the sides of the bowl while the mixer is running. Pour in the melted cocoa butter and continue to heat the bowl, then add the almonds, pistachios, cranberries and diced apricots. Mix at low speed until the consistency is firm.
- Pour the nougat onto the wafer sheet. Cover with the other silicone mat and, using a rolling pin, roll out to a thickness of 1.5 cm. Remove the mat and place the other wafer sheet on the nougat, gently rolling with the rolling pin to ensure it adheres.
- Leave the nougat to dry for 12 hours at room temperature. Trim the edges of the nougat with a serrated knife before cutting into 6 x 2 cm rectangles.
- Soft nougat with aquafaba will keep for up to 3 weeks in a dry place in an airtight container.

Lactose-free
soft caramels

Soft caramel is traditionally made with cream and butter. The dairy products in this recipe can be easily replaced with coconut milk, soya drink and cocoa butter. The taste isn't identical, but this caramel will still appeal to anyone not wanting to consume ingredients containing lactose.

FOR 20 SOFT CARAMELS

DIFFICULTY

Preparation time: 15 min • Resting time: 2 h • Cooking time: 10 min

INGREDIENTS

150 g unrefined cane sugar • 265 g glucose • 75 ml soya drink • 300 ml coconut milk • 70 g trehalose • 45 g Trimoline® (inverted sugar) • 25 g cocoa butter • 4 g fine "fleur de sel" sea salt

EQUIPMENT

1 x 14 x 14 cm stainless steel frame • 1 cooking thermometer • Cellophane (optional)

- Line a baking tray with baking parchment and place the frame on it.
- Pour the unrefined cane sugar and glucose into a saucepan and heat, without stirring, until the mixture becomes a caramel (180°C).
- In another saucepan, bring the soya drink, coconut milk, trehalose and Trimoline® to the boil. Carefully drizzle over the caramel, stirring with a spatula until smooth, then heat until the temperature reaches 112°C on the cooking thermometer.
- Remove the saucepan from the heat and carefully add the cocoa butter and fine "fleur de sel" sea salt. Mix until the cocoa butter has melted and the mixture is smooth.
- Pour the caramel into the frame and leave at room temperature to cool. When the caramel has hardened (about 2 hours), remove it from the frame by running the blade of a knife around the inside edge, then carefully peel off the baking parchment.
- Using a large knife, cut 2 x 7 cm rectangles, then wrap the caramels in cellophane if you wish.
- Soft caramels will keep for up to 3 weeks in a dry place in an airtight container.

Reduced sugar lollipops

FOR 8 LOLLIPOPS

DIFFICULTY

Preparation time: 15 min • Resting time: 20 min • Cooking time: 10 min

COOKED SUGAR SYRUP
200 ml water • 150 g trehalose • 350 g sugar • 150 g glucose

MINT FLAVOURING
2 drops green liquid food colouring • 5 drops natural peppermint flavouring • 1 g citric acid

STRAWBERRY VARIATION
2 drops red liquid food colouring • 5 drops natural strawberry flavouring

EQUIPMENT
2 x 6 cm Ø x 4 mm swirl silicone lollipop moulds • 8 wooden sticks • 1 cooking thermometer

- Place the lollipop moulds on a baking tray lined with baking parchment, then push 1 stick into each mould.

COOKED SUGAR SYRUP
- Pour the water, trehalose and sugar into a saucepan, stir to dissolve the sugar, then bring to the boil. Add the glucose and heat until the temperature reaches 155°C (barley-coloured sugar) on the cooking thermometer.

MINT FLAVOURING
- Add the green food colouring, flavouring and citric acid (1). Gently stir with a spoon until the colour is uniform.

- Remove from the heat and carefully pour into the lollipop moulds (2).
- Wait until the lollipops have cooled completely, about 15 to 20 minutes, before unmoulding (3).
- Reduced sugar lollipops will keep for up to 1 week in a dry place in an airtight container.

STRAWBERRY VARIATION
- Follow the recipe, replacing the green food colouring and peppermint flavouring with the red food colouring and strawberry flavouring.

Homemade chocolate bars
with no white sugar

Although a stone grinder is not a common kitchen accessory, chocolate aficionados will find one very useful. Ideal for anyone embarking on the adventure of making chocolate from cocoa beans (which are becoming increasingly easy to find in shops), a grinder can also be used to make praline.

FOR 6 X 125 G CHOCOLATE BARS

DIFFICULTY

Preparation time: 14 h 50 min

DARK COUVERTURE CHOCOLATE
100 g cocoa butter • 600 g cocoa beans • 300 g coconut blossom sugar

MILK COUVERTURE CHOCOLATE VARIATION
260 g cocoa butter • 150 g cocoa beans • 350 g coconut blossom sugar • 240 g milk powder

EQUIPMENT
1 food processor • 1 stone chocolate grinder • 6 plastic moulds for 125 g bars

COCOA BUTTER

With an almost neutral taste, cocoa butter is a fatty substance with a faint aroma of cocoa that is released after cocoa beans have been ground during the cocoa-powder manufacturing process. It is an ingredient in chocolate.

Homemade chocolate bars with no white sugar

DARK COUVERTURE CHOCOLATE

- Weigh all the ingredients (1). Melt the cocoa butter over a bain-marie.

- Grind the cocoa beans to a fine powder in the food processor. Put the powder obtained into the stone grinder (2) and grind for about 5 minutes.

- Add a quarter of the coconut blossom sugar (about 75 g) (3) then a third of the melted cocoa butter (about 30 g) (4). Continue to grind for 10 minutes before adding another quarter of the sugar and a third of the melted cocoa butter.

- Grind for a further 10 minutes, then add a quarter of the sugar and the last third of the cocoa butter. After 10 minutes, add the last 75 g of sugar. At this stage, the chocolate should have become a very firm paste (5).

- Leave the grinder running for at least 12 hours, until all the ingredients have turned into a very fine chocolate mixture (due to the action of the stones, the grinder does not heat the chocolate as it is forming and the temperature stays below 45°C).

- Remove the chocolate from the grinder and temper it (see pp. 45–48) (6) before filling the plastic bar moulds to the top (7).

- Leave the homemade chocolate bars to harden for 2 hours at room temperature before unmoulding (8).

MILK COUVERTURE CHOCOLATE VARIATION

- Follow the same method as for the dark chocolate, adding the milk powder a little at a time with the coconut blossom sugar and melted cocoa butter.

- Chocolate will keep for up to several months at 20°C in a dry dark place in an airtight container.

GLUTEN-FREE COFFEE AND BUCKWHEAT BITES

SUGAR- AND LACTOSE-FREE COCONUT AND CINNAMON TRUFFLES

Gluten-free buckwheat and coffee bites

FOR 12 BITES

DIFFICULTY
Preparation time: 1 h • **Resting time:** 4 h
• **Cooking time:** 30 min

COFFEE GANACHE
25 g coffee beans • 135 g coconut cream • 100 g dark couverture chocolate 70% • 5 g Trimoline® (inverted sugar)

BUCKWHEAT FEUILLETINE
30 g plant-based margarine at room temperature • 40 g unrefined cane sugar • 30 g egg white • 40 g buckwheat flour

BUCKWHEAT AND PRALINE CRISP
130 g buckwheat feuilletine • 26 g plant-based margarine • 132 g almond and hazelnut praline • 1 pinch salt

CHOCOLATE GLAZE
150 g dark couverture chocolate 70% • 30 ml grapeseed oil

EQUIPMENT
1 conical sieve • 2 piping bags • 1 silicone mould with 12 x 4.5 cm Ø x 2 cm deep imprints • 1 stand mixer • 1 dipping fork • 1 soft acetate guitar sheet • 1 paper cone (see p. 54)

COFFEE GANACHE

- Preheat the oven to 170°C. Place the coffee beans on a baking tray and roast for 10 minutes.
- Pour the coconut cream into a saucepan and add the coffee beans. Bring to the boil, then remove from the heat. Cover and leave to infuse for 1 hour.
- Bring the cream and coffee beans to the boil, then strain over the chocolate. Stir with a silicone spatula to form a ganache. Add the Trimoline® and stir until smooth. Pour into 1 piping bag and fill the imprints halfway up. Leave to harden in the freezer for 1 hour.

BUCKWHEAT FEUILLETINE

- Line a baking tray with baking parchment.
- In a bowl, whisk together the margarine and unrefined cane sugar until creamy, then fold in the egg white and flour. Stir just until just smooth.
- Pour onto the baking tray and roll it out thinly. Bake for 20 minutes, leave to cool on the baking tray, then break it into pieces.

BUCKWHEAT AND PRALINE CRISP

- Mix the buckwheat feuilletine, plant-based margarine, praline and salt in the bowl of a mixer fitted with a paddle attachment at low speed until smooth. Using a piping bag or a spoon, fill the moulds to the top with the ganache. Flatten with a spatula and leave to harden in the freezer for 1 hour.

CHOCOLATE GLAZE

- Melt the chocolate with the grapeseed oil over a bain-marie. Cool to 27°C.
- Unmould the bites then, using the fork, dip them one by one into the glaze while they are still cold. Run them over the rim of the bowl to remove the excess, then place on a baking tray lined with the soft acetate guitar sheet. Refrigerate for 1 hour.
- Fill the paper cone with chocolate glaze and pipe fine lines across the tops of the bites. Bites will keep for up to 5 days in a dry place in an airtight container at room temperature.

Sugar- and lactose-free
coconut and cinnamon truffles

FOR 35 TRUFFLES

DIFFICULTY

Preparation time: 40 min • Refrigeration time: 1 h 20 min • Cooking time: 5 min

GANACHE
150 g dark couverture chocolate 70% • 150 g coconut cream • 1 g ground cinnamon • 10 ml maple syrup • 10 ml coconut oil

COATING
250 g dark couverture chocolate 70% • 100 g desiccated coconut

EQUIPMENT
1 cooking thermometer • 1 piping bag • 1 plain 10 mm Ø nozzle • 1 pair thin latex gloves • 1 round dipping fork

GANACHE
- Melt the chocolate to 45°C over a bain-marie. At the same time, heat the coconut cream, cinnamon and maple syrup in a saucepan to 45°C, then pour it over the melted chocolate. Using a silicone spatula, stir to form a ganache, then add the coconut oil off the heat. Stir until the ganache is smooth.
- Cover with cling film in direct contact with the ganache and chill in the refrigerator for 15 to 20 minutes or until it begins to thicken.
- Stir the ganache with a spatula until it thickens. Fill the piping bag fitted with the nozzle.
- Pipe 2 cm diameter balls onto a baking tray lined with baking parchment. Refrigerate for 1 hour.
- Wearing gloves, roll each truffle between your hands until nice and round.

COATING
- Temper the dark chocolate (see pp. 45–48).
- Using the fork, dip the ganache balls one by one into the tempered chocolate, then immediately roll them in the desiccated coconut. Leave to cool in the coconut.
- Truffles will keep for up to 1 week in an airtight container at room temperature.

CHEF'S TIP

If the truffles become too soft after shaping, place them in the refrigerator for 10 to 15 minutes before dipping.

Decorations and artistic centrepieces

Almond paste
figures

You can buy sets of modelling tools for sculpting that can also be used to shape almond paste. If you don't have a set of tools, you can use things you have at home: a spoon, a knife, piping nozzles, etc. to make animals, flowers, fruit, vegetables, etc.

FOR 3 X 50 G FIGURES

DIFFICULTY
Preparation time: 20 min

INGREDIENTS
60 g royal icing (see p. 282) • Black liquid food colouring

- - -

150 g almond paste (see p. 42) • Red liquid food colouring • Orange liquid food colouring
• Black liquid food colouring

EQUIPMENT
1 pair thin latex gloves • 2 paper cones (see p. 54) • 1 set modelling tools for almond paste
(or 1 small knife and 1 plain 6 mm Ø round nozzle)

CHEF'S TIPS

Remember to wear gloves when adding liquid food colouring. • Water-soluble, water-based colourings can be used for colouring sugar and almond-paste-based preparations and for macaron batter, pastillage, cakes, etc. • Wrap the pieces of almond paste you are not working on in cling film to prevent them from drying out.

- Prepare the almond paste.

ROYAL ICING

- Prepare a ½ recipe for royal icing, then take 1 tablespoon of the mixture and place in 1 paper cone. Colour 1 tablespoon of royal icing black for the eyes, then transfer it to the other cone. Set aside at room temperature.

RABBIT

- Take 50 g of almond paste. Wearing gloves, colour it with a few drops of red colouring and mix until the colour is homogeneous.
- Roll the almond paste into a cylinder about 1.5 cm in diameter and 13 cm long.
- Cut a 1.5 cm piece for the hind legs, tail, cheeks, nose and mouth; 4.5 cm for the head and 7 cm for the body.
- Divide the 1.5 cm piece into seven pieces: three slightly larger pieces to be shaped into cones for the hind legs and tail; two slightly smaller ones for the cheeks, and the last two significantly smaller ones for the nose and mouth. Shape into balls.

FOR THE HEAD

- Slightly flatten the balls for the cheeks and mouth. Place the three pieces side by side and place the nose on top, pressing a little so that the four pieces stick together. Using a pointed tool, make three little indentations in each cheek for the rabbit's whiskers.
- Using the 4.5 cm piece, first shape it into a ball in the hollow of your palm, then shape to a point.
- Using a knife, divide the pointed part from the rounded part in the following proportions: one third for the pointed part to make the ears and two thirds for the rounded part to make the rabbit's head.
- Place it on the work surface and slice the pointed part in half lengthways. Lay the cut part face down on the work surface and use a tool to create an indentation in the centre of each ear.

FOR THE BODY

- Shape the remaining 7 cm piece into a ball. Make it into the shape of a carrot.
- Place the wide, rounded part on the work surface. Fold and bring the thinner part forward. Cut the thin 1 cm part in half to make the front legs.
- Use a finger to make an indentation at the top of the rounded part and place the head there.
- Place the hind legs on either side of the rabbit's body and the tail at the back. Mark fingers on all four paws.

FINAL ASSEMBLY

- Place the cheek-mouth-nose section on the rounded part of the head. Use a round-tipped tool to make two indentations to mark where the eyes will go. To finish the eyes, use a paper cone to pipe a dot of white royal icing, then pipe a small dot of black royal icing on top. ▸

DECORATIONS AND ARTISTIC CENTREPIECES

Almond paste figures

FISH

- Colour 50 g of almond paste with a few drops of orange food colouring.
- Roll the almond paste into a cylinder about 1.5 cm in diameter and 13 cm long.
- Cut off two slices, each about 0.5 cm. One slice will be used for the dorsal fin, and the other slice – divided into three equal pieces – will be used for the pectoral fins and the mouth.
- Shape the dorsal fin into a carrot shape first, then flatten it. Turn one side up a little and score a fan pattern on it. Shape the pectoral fins in the same way. For the mouth, form a slightly flattened ball.
- Using the rest of the almond paste, first form a ball in the hollow of your palm, then shape to a point. Separate a pointed part from the rounded part in the following proportions: one third for the pointed part and two thirds for the rounded part, which will be elongated a little. Place it on the work surface and cut the pointed part lengthways in half to form the tail. Slightly flatten the two sides of the tail, then use a knife to score a fan pattern. Pivot the tail a quarter turn in relation to the fish's body so that the tail fins are straight. Curl the fin to give it movement.
- Using a sculpting tool, or the back of a knife, make a mark to differentiate the head from the body, then use a half-moon-shaped tool (or a small piping nozzle) to create the scales on the body of the fish.
- Attach the small, flattened ball to form the mouth, then use a tool to make two indentations where the eyes will go. Use the paper cones to pipe a dot of white royal icing, then a dot of black royal icing on top.
- Finish the fish by attaching the dorsal and pectoral fins.

ELEPHANT

- Colour 50 g of almond paste with a few drops of black food colouring to obtain a homogeneous grey colour.
- Roll the almond paste into a cylinder about 1.5 cm in diameter and 13 cm long.
- Cut two thin slices about 2 to 3 mm thick to form elephant's ears.
- Shape into balls and flatten, creating a thicker edge on one side for each.
- Divide the rest of the cylinder in half; two thirds for the body and one third for the head.

FOR THE BODY

- Make a 1 cm slit in the two ends of the cylinder to form the legs, then fold the cylinder back on itself in an arch, spreading the cut ends slightly apart. Position the body on the legs.

FOR THE HEAD

- Shape the almond paste into an elongated pear. Score the elongated part horizontally with a knife to create the folds of its trunk. Use a round-tipped tool to make two indentations to mark where the eyes will go. Using the paper cones, pipe a dot of white royal icing into the hollows, then a dot of black royal icing on top.
- Attach the head to the body, then attach the ears.
- Almond paste figures will keep for about 1 week in an airtight container at room temperature.

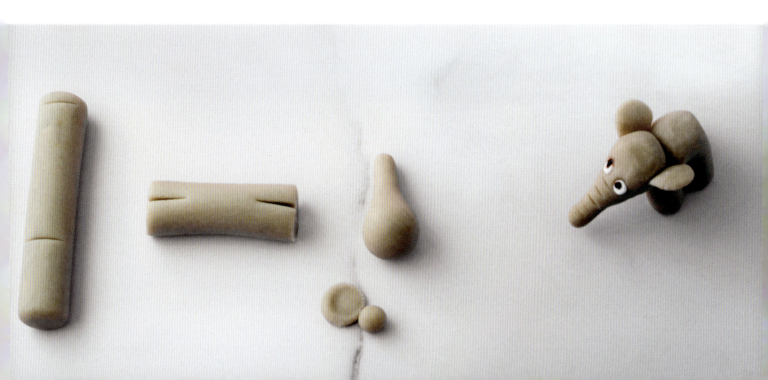

Nougatine

FOR 950 G OF NOUGATINE

DIFFICULTY ◯◯

Preparation time: 30 min • **Cooking time:** 20 min

INGREDIENTS
240 g flaked almonds • 10 g butter

COOKED SUGAR SYRUP
80 ml water • 320 g sugar • 320 g glucose

VARIATION WITH SESAME SEEDS
160 g white sesame seeds • 80 g black sesame seeds

EQUIPMENT
1 cooking thermometer • 2 silicone mats • 1 nougatine roller (or 1 rolling pin) • Biscuit cutters of your choice

- Preheat the oven to 170°C. Place the almonds on a baking tray and roast for 10 minutes. Set aside.
- Turn the oven down to 140°C and return the empty baking tray to the middle of the oven in case you need to soften the nougatine later.

COOKED SUGAR SYRUP

- Pour the water and sugar into a saucepan and stir to dissolve the sugar. Bring to the boil, then add the glucose. Heat to a light caramel colour, about 160°C (barley-coloured sugar) on the cooking thermometer.
- Carefully add the flaked almonds (1), then the butter and mix until the almonds are well coated.
- Pour onto 1 silicone mat and cover with the other mat. Carefully roll it out using the nougatine roller (2) to a thickness of 2 to 4 mm depending on what it will be used for (or press firmly with a rolling pin).
- While the nougatine is still hot, use a knife or biscuit cutters to cut out the desired shapes (3).
- While still hot, the shapes can be folded around a container or moulds to give them their final shape.
- Once the pieces are finished, leave to cool before placing the nougatine in an airtight container in a dry place.
- If stacking the pieces, separate the layers with baking parchment.

VARIATION WITH SESAME SEEDS

- Replace the flaked almonds with sesame seeds and proceed in the same way.

CHEF'S TIPS

Don't hesitate to reheat the nougatine for a few minutes on the baking tray if it becomes too hard.
• Shapes cut to a thickness of about 4 mm can be used as bases or structures for artistic centrepieces. Thinner shapes (about 2 mm thick) can be used as decorative elements to be placed on an artistic centrepiece.

Pastillage

Biscuit cutters can make beautiful effects on decorative pieces. Made of plastic, stainless steel or tinplate, nowadays, there are all sorts available. Some plastic models have a plunger or pusher for cutting or tracing a pattern onto very delicate surfaces. The plunger makes it easier to extract the cut shape, preventing it from getting damaged. Stainless steel or tinplate models are ideal for cutting out biscuits, cookies, etc.

FOR 520 G OF PASTILLAGE

DIFFICULTY

Preparation time: 30 min • **Refrigeration time:** 30 min • **Resting time:** 24 h • **Cooking time:** 2 min

INGREDIENTS

20 ml cold water • 4 g powdered gelatine • 450 g icing sugar • 25 g potato starch • 25 ml distilled vinegar • Liquid food colouring (optional)

EQUIPMENT

1 stand mixer • Decorative plastic cutters (flowers of assorted shapes and sizes, four-leaf clovers, butterflies, petals, etc.) • 1 Silpain® mat

- Prepare the gelatine mass. Pour the water over the gelatine in a bowl and leave to hydrate for 30 minutes in the refrigerator.
- Sift the icing sugar and potato starch together, then tip into the bowl of the stand mixer fitted with a paddle attachment.
- Bring the vinegar to the boil, then remove from the heat and add the gelatine mass. Stir to dissolve and immediately add to the bowl. Mix on low speed until a dough forms (about 4 minutes).
- Place the pastillage paste on the work surface and smear out in front of you with the palm of your hand (fraser) (1) several times until the dough is smooth and no longer grainy.
- To make decorations, thinly roll out some of the pastillage to a thickness of about 1 mm (2). Use the biscuit cutters to cut out the desired shapes (3) then carefully place them, using your hands or a plastic spatula, on a baking tray lined with the Silpain® mat. Leave to dry out for at least 24 hours at room temperature.
- For a curved effect, gently place the cut piece around a rolling pin, in a bowl or other containers, and leave to dry out.
- Wrap any unused pastillage in cling film covered with a damp cloth. It will keep in the refrigerator for up to 1 week.
- Pastillage can be coloured with 1 to 4 drops of food colouring as you work it; the amount depends on the desired brightness, or it can be painted with an airbrush.

Pressed sugar, poured sugar and royal icing

Easy to mould and unmould when using silicone or stainless steel moulds, pressed sugar lends itself to a wide variety of shapes. Once cooked and dried, it stays solid for a very long time and is highly resistant to damp and humidity. Small elements can be used to decorate cakes or sweeten coffee, while larger creations are used as bases for displays.

Poured sugar is often used as a base for artistic centrepieces because it is solid and can support the weight of the various pieces that make up the final composition. It can also be used to make small decorative pieces or to fill PVC tubes.

Royal icing is an essential preparation that lends itself to a number of uses. It can be used when it comes to assembling the various parts of an artistic decoration or as a decorative element in its own right. When delicately and decoratively piped, it makes the result look elegant and light.

PRESSED SUGAR

FOR 500 G OF PRESSED SUGAR

DIFFICULTY

Preparation time: 5 min • Cooking time: 30 min

INGREDIENTS
500 g sugar • 20 ml distilled vinegar • 5 drops liquid food colouring of your choice (optional)

EQUIPMENT
1 x 12 cm Ø x 1 cm high silicone mould with 2 imprints

POURED SUGAR

FOR 700 G OF POURED SUGAR

DIFFICULTY

Preparation time: 15 min • Resting time: 1 or 2 h • Cooking time: 15 min

INGREDIENTS
200 ml water • 550 g sugar • 175 g glucose • 5 drops of liquid food colouring of your choice

EQUIPMENT
Stainless steel entremets rings or silicone moulds • 1 silicone mat • 1 cooking thermometer

ROYAL ICING

FOR 125 G OF ROYAL ICING

DIFFICULTY

Preparation time: 5 min

INGREDIENTS
100 g icing sugar • 20 g egg white • 5 ml distilled vinegar

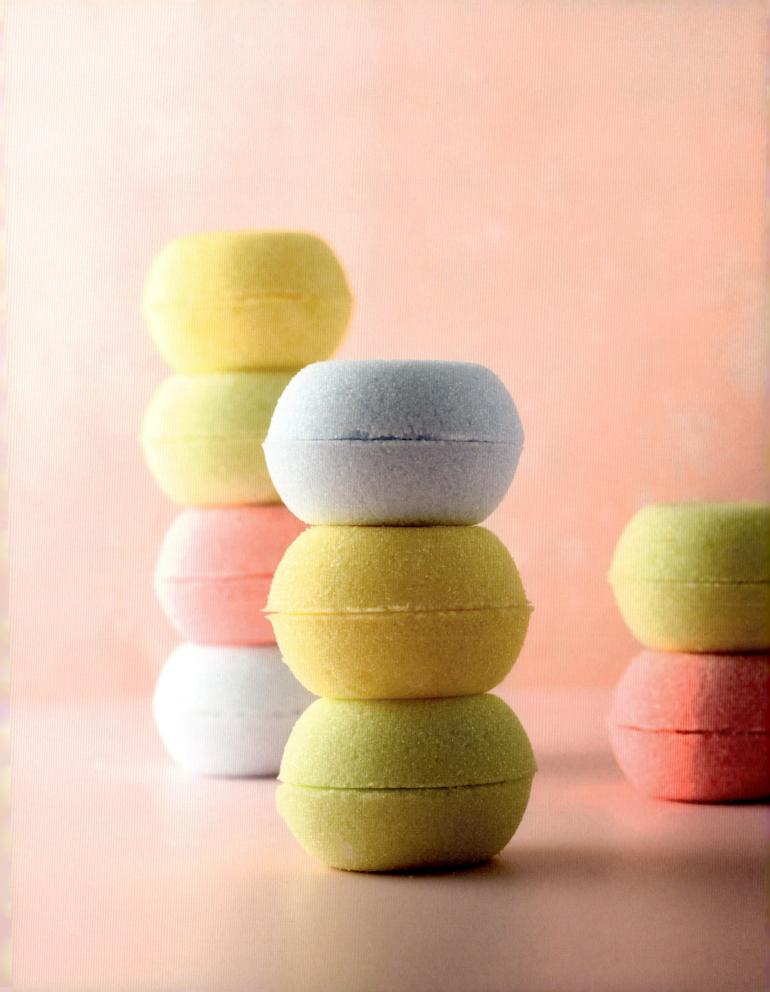

Pressed sugar, poured sugar and royal icing

PRESSED SUGAR

- Preheat the oven to 100°C.
- Pour the sugar into a bowl, followed by the vinegar (and food colouring, if using). Mix with a spoon (1) until all the sugar has been moistened.
- Fill the mould imprints with the moistened sugar using a spoon, pressing hard first on the sides, then gradually towards the centre so that the sugar is well packed (2).
- Place the base of a bowl or a flat-bottomed object on top and press down firmly to finish packing the sugar. Heat for 30 minutes, or leave to harden for 1 to 2 hours at room temperature.
- Gently unmould the pressed sugar (3). It can be stored at room temperature.
- Elements made of pressed sugar will keep almost indefinitely in a dry place or in a container with calcium chloride.

POURED SUGAR

- Place the entremets rings or silicone moulds on a baking tray lined with the silicone mat.
- Pour the water and sugar into a saucepan and stir to dissolve the sugar. Bring to the boil, then add the glucose. Heat until the temperature reaches 160°C (barley-coloured sugar) on the cooking thermometer.
- Add the colouring and stir with the probe of the thermometer until evenly coloured, then leave to cool slightly so that the bubbles disappear.
- Carefully pour into the moulds. Leave to cool for 1 or 2 hours (depending on the size of the pieces) before unmoulding.
- Elements made of poured sugar will keep almost indefinitely in a dry place or in a container with calcium chloride.

ROYAL ICING

- Sift the icing sugar into a bowl. Add the egg white and vinegar, then whisk until smooth and supple. If the royal icing mixture is too hard, add a little egg white to soften it. If it is too liquid, add 1 teaspoon of icing sugar.
- Royal icing will keep for 1 day covered with a damp cloth, then wrapped in cling film at room temperature. Once piped and dried, it will keep almost indefinitely.

CHEF'S TIP

A fan can help cool poured sugar.

Pulled sugar

FOR 1 KG OF PULLED SUGAR

DIFFICULTY ◯◯◯

Preparation time: 40 min • Cooking time: 15 min

INGREDIENTS
280 ml water • 500 g sugar • 350 g glucose • 5 drops tartaric acid • 3 drops liquid orange food colouring

EQUIPMENT
1 cooking thermometer • 2 silicone mats • 1 sugar lamp • 1 pair latex sugar work gloves • 1 chef's blowtorch • 1 silicone leaf pulled sugar mould

PULLED SUGAR

- Pour the water and sugar into a saucepan and stir to dissolve the sugar.
- Bring to the boil and skim off any impurities with a skimmer or tablespoon. Add the glucose and allow the temperature to reach 140°C (soft crack) on the cooking thermometer without stirring. Add the tartaric acid and heat rapidly until the temperature reaches 155°C (barley-coloured sugar).
- Carefully pour half of the hot cooked sugar syrup onto 1 silicone mat (1).
- Add the colouring to the remaining cooked sugar syrup in the saucepan and stir with the probe of the thermometer until evenly coloured. Carefully pour over the other silicone mat.
- Allow the two cooked sugar masses to cool to about 80°C (the cooked sugar should be malleable). Turn the two masses of sugar over so that they cool evenly.
- Turn on the sugar lamp.
- Wearing gloves, take the outer edges of the uncoloured cooked sugar first and fold them towards the centre. Gradually shape into a ball that keeps its shape. Place the resulting sugar under the sugar lamp. Repeat with the coloured cooked sugar. The texture of the two balls should be similar.

MAKING SATIN FINISH PULLED SUGAR

- Pull the cooked sugar to make it shiny: shape the uncoloured cooked sugar into a rope, then take each end and pull it (2) to a length of about 30 to 40 cm. Fold it in half (3). Repeat the operation about 20 times until you hear the sugar crackle and the cooked sugar is opaque and white. Put it back under the sugar lamp to keep it warm and so that the satin finish white sugar stays malleable. Repeat with the coloured cooked sugar.

PULLED SUGAR RIBBON

- Make a rope with the satin finish white sugar and another with the satin finish coloured sugar. The two ropes must be the same length and thickness.
- Place the two ropes side by side, touching each other, on the mat. Pull the sugar mass to lengthen it as evenly as possible, then, when it is about 30 cm long, fold it in half so that the inner edges stick together (4). Use scissors to trim the ends of the sugar to make it easier to fold (5).
- Repeat the operation (pulling and folding) twice more (6), then pull so that the ribbon is about 25 cm long (7). Place the resulting ribbon on the silicone mat.
- Heat the blade of a knife with the blowtorch, then cut the ribbon at approximately 12 cm intervals (8). Pass the pieces one by one under the sugar lamp to warm them slightly, then gently fold each ribbon to form a bow (9).

▶

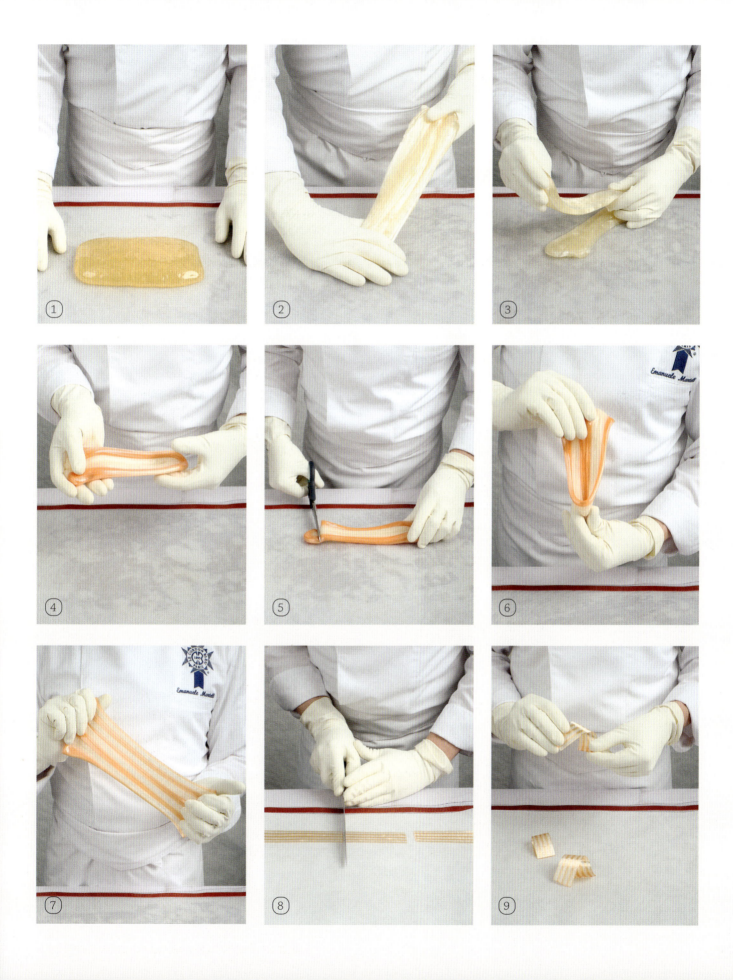

PULLED SUGAR LEAVES

- Wearing gloves, under the sugar lamp, with the thumb and forefinger of each hand, pull a piece of satin finish pulled sugar laterally to form a thin edge. Using your thumb and forefinger, gently pull on the stretched thin edge of the satin finish pulled sugar. Cut out a rounded shape and immediately place it in the silicone leaf mould. Cover with the other half of the mould and press down firmly. Remove the leaf from the mould and place it on the silicone mat. Leave to cool.

PULLED SUGAR SPIRAL AND RING

- Wearing gloves, and under the sugar lamp, gently pull a small amount of the satin finish sugar with the thumb and forefinger of both hands to lengthen the sugar evenly. Gently wrap it around a small cylinder, then remove the spiral before placing it on the silicone mat.

- For the ring, instead of rolling the satin finish sugar around a cylinder, pull it to a length of about 35 cm, then wrap it around a stainless steel entremets ring and join the two ends to form a ring. Leave to harden for a few minutes, then remove the ring.

PULLED SUGAR ROSE

- Wearing gloves, under the sugar lamp, with the thumb and forefinger of each hand, pull a piece of satin finish pulled sugar laterally to form a thin edge. Using your thumb and forefinger, gently pull on the stretched thin edge of the satin finish pulled sugar to take the shape of the thumb. Cut with scissors, then fold the outer edges to make the centre of the rose. Place on the silicone mat.

- Using your thumb and forefinger, take another small piece of the satin finish sugar so that it takes the shape of your thumb. Twist and pull the sugar, then cut with scissors. Place the rounded part around the base of the centre of the rose. If necessary, heat the base of the petals with the blowtorch so that they are soft enough to stick to the centre. Repeat the operation, arranging each rose petal in a staggered pattern. Make two or three rows of petals to create the rose. Leave to cool on the silicone mat.

CHEF'S TIPS

Pulled sugar elements will keep in an airtight container on baking parchment with a dehydrating agent such as calcium chloride in it. • Use longer latex sugar work gloves to avoid burning your hands and, above all, to prevent the sweat from your hands coming into contact with the sugar, which could recrystallise it.
• Take care not to pull the sugar too much: pulling and folding can be done about 20 times. • If the satin finish sugar cools too much, it can be reheated in the microwave for a maximum of 10 seconds; any longer and the sugar will begin to liquefy. • Don't hesitate to put the cooked sugar back under the sugar lamp at each stage before working it. • Ribbons can be made using several ropes of cooked sugar: pretty effects can be made by combining satin finish and non-satin finish, coloured and non-coloured ropes of cooked sugar.

Valentine's Day
centrepiece

FOR 1 VALENTINE'S DAY CENTREPIECE

DIFFICULTY ☐☐☐

Preparation time: 1 h 35 min • **Resting time:** 13 h 30 min • **Cooking time:** 1 h 5 min

INGREDIENTS
520 g pastillage (see p. 280) • 300 g white pressed sugar (see p. 282) • 200 g pulled sugar (see p. 286) • 125 g royal icing (see p. 282) • Poured sugar (see p. 282) • 2 drops of red liquid food colouring

EQUIPMENT
2 heart-shaped biscuit cutters 12 and 8 cm Ø • Small heart biscuit cutters • 1 half-sphere silicone mould 4 cm Ø • 1 silicone mould with 6 x 6 cm Ø and 1 cm high imprints • Silicone heart moulds in various sizes • 1 paper cone (see p. 54) • 1 gold cardboard cake board 16 cm Ø for the assembly

---

CHEF'S TIP

Elements made of pastillage and pulled sugar are extremely fragile and break very easily. Don't hesitate to make a few extra elements as replacements.

Valentine's Day centrepiece

DAY 1
PASTILLAGE

- Prepare the pastillage. Roll out to a thickness of 1 or 2 mm, then place the small heart biscuit cutter with the large heart around it (1). Cut out two heart outlines and place them carefully in two bowls to curve them (2). Cut out several small hearts, then place them in the silicone half-sphere mould to curve them. Leave to rest overnight.

DAY 2
POURED SUGAR

- Prepare half a recipe of poured sugar. Set aside 2 tablespoons of it in a semi-liquid state to use as glue.

- Colour the remaining poured sugar red and carefully pour into the imprints of the 6 cm diameter silicone moulds and hearts (3). Leave to cool for at least 1½ hours at room temperature before removing the discs and hearts from the moulds.

PRESSED SUGAR

- Prepare the pressed sugar, then make a pressed sugar disc 12 cm in diameter and 1 cm high. Heat or dry as instructed.

PULLED SUGAR

- Prepare the pulled sugar and make at least two rings (see p. 288). Place them carefully on a baking tray lined with baking parchment.

ROYAL ICING

- Prepare the royal icing. Put a small amount in a paper cone to stick the various elements together.

ASSEMBLY

- Once all the elements are dry or cold, unmould them and group them together on a baking tray lined with baking parchment before assembling (except for the pulled sugar rings) (4).

- Place the pressed sugar disc on the cardboard cake board. Pipe a dot of royal icing in the centre, then add a disc of red poured sugar (5).

- Gently, using the tip of a knife or a small spoon, put a little of the reserved semi-liquid poured sugar on to the pastillage hearts and glue them around the pressed sugar disc. Next, carefully attach the two open hearts, then a red poured sugar heart at an angle to ensure that the pastillage sticks firmly (6).

- Continue adding elements by very gently using the semi-liquid poured sugar to attach the two pulled sugar rings (7), then a few small poured sugar hearts (8).

- Remove the cardboard cake board. This Valentine's Day centrepiece will keep for up to 3 or 4 days in a dry place or, ideally, for up to 1 or 2 months under a bell jar with calcium chloride granules.

Easter egg

FOR 1 EASTER EGG

DIFFICULTY ○○○

Preparation time: 2 h • Resting time: 15 h • Cooking time: 22 min

INGREDIENTS

200 g pastillage (see p. 280) • 500 g tempered dark couverture chocolate 70% (see pp. 45–48)
• 950 g sesame seed nougatine (see variation p. 278) • 150 g royal icing (see p. 282) • Yellow liquid food colouring

EQUIPMENT

Pastillage: 1 small flower biscuit cutter • 1 small butterfly biscuit cutter
Chocolate: 1 cooking thermometer • 1 clean polycarbonate half-egg mould (18 x 12 x 6.5 cm) • 1 pastry brush
• 1 pair cotton gloves • 1 round stainless steel mould (8 cm Ø)
Nougatine: 1 x 8 x 8 cm and 2 cm high stainless steel mould • 2 silicone mats • 1 pair thin latex gloves
• 1 clean polycarbonate half-egg mould (18 x 12 x 6.5 cm)
Royal icing: 1 piping bag • 1 plain 6 mm Ø nozzle
Assembly: 2 paper cones (see p. 54) • 1 chef's blowtorch • 1 square cardboard cake board

CHEF'S TIP

A cardboard cake board helps artistic centrepieces to remain stable while being assembled, and its colour can also play a decorative role. It also makes it easier to transport and handle after being assembled.

Easter egg

DAY 1
PASTILLAGE
- Prepare the pastillage. Cut out flowers and butterflies and leave to dry overnight.

DARK CHOCOLATE
- Brush a thin layer of chocolate into the half-egg mould, then pour two relatively thick layers into it, one almost immediately after the other. Tap the mould on the work surface to remove any air bubbles and turn it upside down to drain off the excess chocolate (see p. 53, steps 2 and 3); you should have an outer shell of chocolate now. Scrape the top of the mould to ensure a clean edge. Leave to harden for 1 hour, then, wearing cotton gloves (to avoid leaving marks on the chocolate), unmould it and place the half-shell on a baking tray lined with baking parchment.
- For the round base, fill the 8 cm mould with the dark chocolate and leave to harden overnight at room temperature. Unmould onto the baking tray with the half-shell.

DAY 2
NOUGATINE
- Prepare the sesame seed nougatine. Place the 8 cm square mould on a baking tray lined with the silicone mat, then fill with the hot nougatine (1). Leave to cool for at least 2 hours at room temperature.
- Preheat the oven to 140°C. Warm the remaining nougatine in the oven on a baking tray lined with a silicone mat. Wear latex gloves to roll out the nougatine to a 20 x 25 cm sheet, about 3 mm thick, then line the half-egg mould with it (2). Carefully, and while still hot, trim the edges with scissors to neaten (3). Leave the nougatine to cool for about 15 minutes.
- Unmould the base and the nougatine half-egg and place them on the baking tray with the half-shell and the chocolate disc.

ROYAL ICING
- Prepare the royal icing. Take a tablespoon of royal icing and colour it yellow. Put it in a paper cone and set aside at room temperature. Fill the piping bag with the remaining royal icing and set aside.

ASSEMBLY
- Place the pastillage elements on the baking tray with the other elements for assembling (4).
- Fill 1 paper cone with tempered dark chocolate.
- Place the nougatine half-shell at an angle in the polycarbonate mould so that it stays in place. Pipe a line of tempered dark chocolate around the edge (5) then, wearing gloves, stick it to the chocolate half-shell (6). Leave to harden for 15 to 20 minutes at room temperature.
- Attach the nougatine square to the cardboard cake board with a dot of chocolate. Pipe another dot in the middle, then place the chocolate disc in the centre. Pipe a ball of chocolate in the centre, then place the egg on top (7). Hold the egg in place for a few minutes so that it adheres properly to the base.
- Once the egg is stuck to the base, pipe small dots of royal icing around the seam of the egg to decorate it and reinforce it (8). Pipe small dots around the base of the egg where it sits on the chocolate disc.
- Pipe a dot of yellow royal icing in the middle of the pastillage flowers. Leave to dry for about 15 minutes. Attach the flowers and butterflies to the egg harmoniously (9).
- This egg will keep for up to 1 week in a dry place at room temperature.

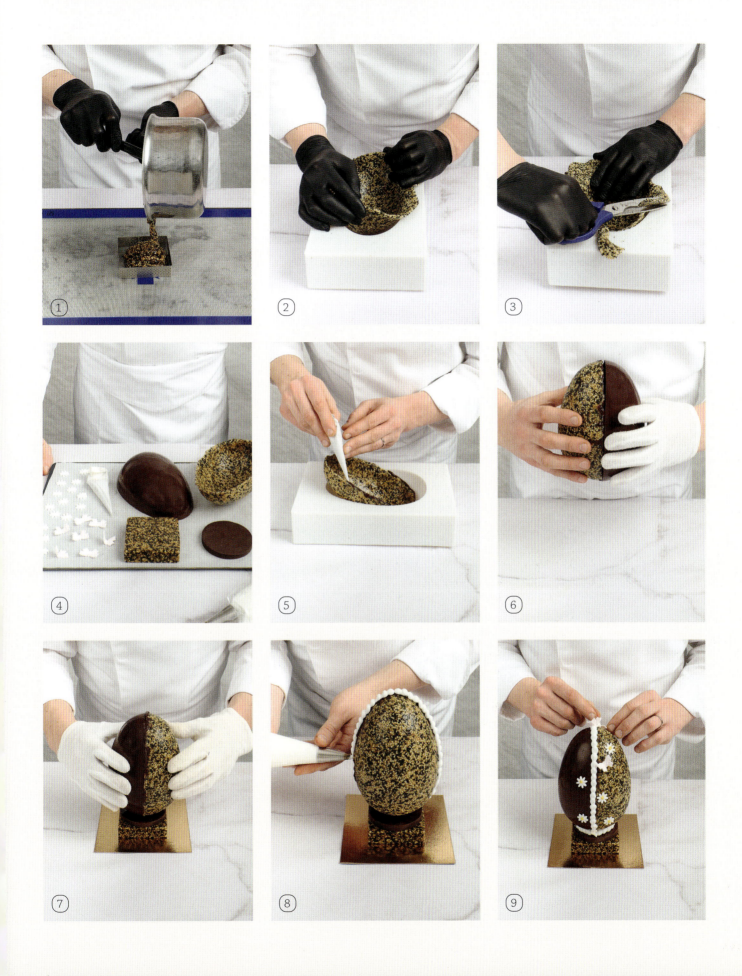

Christmas tree

FOR 1 CHRISTMAS TREE

DIFFICULTY

Preparation time: 2 or 3 h • Resting time: 3 or 4 h • Freezing time: 10 to 20 min

INGREDIENTS
600 g dark couverture chocolate 70% • Apple-green velvet-effect cocoa butter spray colouring
• Pastillage snowflakes (see p. 280) prepared the day before

EQUIPMENT
1 cooking thermometer • 1 x 6 cm Ø x 2 cm high stainless steel ring • 1 x 4 cm Ø x 4 cm high stainless steel ring
• 1 x 8 cm Ø stainless steel ring • 1 pair thin latex gloves • Polycarbonate half-sphere mould 3 cm Ø with 25 imprints
• Polycarbonate half-sphere mould 4 cm Ø with 6 imprints • Polycarbonate half-sphere mould 6 cm Ø with 2 imprints
• 1 chef's blowtorch • 1 paper cone (see p. 54)

CHEF'S TIPS

The velvety effect of the tree is achieved by the contrast in temperature between the sprayed cocoa butter and the very cold chocolate. • Make sure that the temperature of the chocolate does not fall more than 1°C below the tempering temperature. Keep a bain-marie on hand to warm it up for a few seconds if necessary, and stir the chocolate before using again.

Christmas tree

CHOCOLATE ELEMENTS

- Temper the dark chocolate (see pp. 45–48). Set aside about 100 g in a bowl for sticking. Line the bottoms of the 6, 4 and 8 cm stainless steel rings with cling film, then place them on a baking tray. Fill the 4 and 6 cm rings completely with the tempered dark chocolate, then the 8 cm ring with a layer about 3 mm thick.

- Leave to harden for 2 or 3 hours at room temperature, then, wearing gloves, unmould and place the pieces on a baking tray lined with baking parchment.

- Mould the tempered chocolate in the half-sphere moulds (see p. 53, steps 1 to 3).

- Leave to harden at room temperature for about 1 hour, then, wearing gloves, unmould and place the pieces on a baking tray lined with baking parchment.

ASSEMBLY

- Lightly heat the base of a saucepan and put it on the work surface, bottom up. Take two half-spheres of the same size, place the flat side on the bottom of the saucepan and gently rotate them in small circles (1). Stick the half-spheres together to form a ball and place the ball on the baking parchment. Continue until all the balls have been made.

- Gather all the ingredients for the tree on a baking tray lined with baking parchment (2).

- Using the blowtorch, lightly heat the surface of the 6 cm base, then place the 4 cm trunk in the centre (3). Heat and stick the 8 cm disc to the centre of the trunk (4). Place the base on the work surface and leave to harden for a few minutes to ensure it is stable.

- Lightly dip a 6 cm ball into the reserved bowl of tempered dark chocolate. Place it on the edge of the disc. Then, taking balls of different sizes, dip them and attach them to the disc, piling them up. Wait a few minutes between each layer to make sure the chocolate has hardened and the tree is stable (5) (6).

- Keep going up until all the balls have been used and assembled harmoniously (7).

- Carefully place the tree in the freezer for 10 to 20 minutes (or refrigerate for 30 minutes), then place it on baking parchment on the work surface.

- Spray the colour evenly all over the tree to give a velvety effect (8). Leave to harden for a few minutes. Then, use the cone filled with tempered dark chocolate to attach small pastillage snowflakes.

Artistic centrepiece

FOR 1 ARTISTIC CENTREPIECE

DIFFICULTY ♙♙♙

Preparation time: 2 h 15 min • **Resting time:** 12 h • **Cooking time:** 55 min

INGREDIENTS

520 g pastillage (see p. 280) • 500 g tempered dark couverture chocolate 70% (see pp. 45–48) • 950 g sesame seed nougatine (see p. 278) • 500 g pulled sugar (see p. 286) • Gold leaf (optional) • 700 g poured sugar (see p. 282) • Yellow liquid food colouring

EQUIPMENT

Pastillage: Butterfly cutters: butterfly wings, flowers and four-leaf clovers in various sizes • 1 round mould
Chocolate: 1 cooking thermometer • 1 piping bag • 1 x 12 cm Ø x 2 cm high silicone mould with 2 imprints • 1 x 6 cm Ø stainless steel ring • 1 x 10 cm Ø x 3.5 cm high stainless steel ring
Poured sugar: 1 silicone mat • 1 food processor • 1 flexible PVC tube 3.5 cm Ø x 18 to 20 cm long • 1 pair latex sugar work gloves • 1x 12 cm Ø x 0.5 cm high stainless steel ring • 3 x 8 cm Ø savarin moulds • 1 chef's blowtorch
Nougatine: 1 x 12 cm Ø x 2 cm high silicone mould • 1 circular mould
Assembly: 2 silicone mats • Sandpaper • 1 x 16 cm Ø gold cardboard cake board • 1 spirit level • 1 small wooden rolling pin

---

CHEF'S TIPS

Before creating an artistic centrepiece, make sketches to work out its harmonious visual impact and what elements need to be prepared in advance (1). • Always make a few extra parts to replace any that may break. • Keep the excess poured sugar for sticking the sugar elements and pastillage to the centrepiece in a container that can be heated briefly in the microwave or in a saucepan. • Wait a few minutes between sticking the various decorative elements so that the poured sugar has time to harden. • Make sure that the temperature of the chocolate does not fall more than 1°C below the tempering temperature. Keep a bain-marie on hand to warm it up for a few seconds if necessary, and stir the chocolate before using again.

Artistic centrepiece

DAY 1
PASTILLAGE

- Prepare the pastillage. Cut out butterflies, butterfly wings, flowers and four-leaf clovers (flat and curved) of various sizes.
- Cut four strips of pastillage 0.5 cm thick, 2 cm wide and 25 cm long, with the ends cut at an angle, then curve them around a circular mould. Leave to dry overnight on a baking tray lined with baking parchment.

CHOCOLATE

- For the ring, place the 6 cm stainless steel ring surrounded by baking parchment in the centre of the silicone mould. Use the piping bag to pipe the chocolate all around it (2). At the same time, pipe and fill the 10 cm stainless steel ring to make the base. Leave the moulds to harden overnight at room temperature, then unmould.
- Set aside the remaining tempered dark chocolate for sticking the chocolate the next day.

POURED SUGAR

- Prepare the poured sugar and colour it yellow. Pour about 100 g of it onto the silicone mat. Leave to cool, then coarsely crush in a food processor and sieve it to keep only the larger pieces. Set aside.
- Seal one end of the tube with adhesive tape and then, wearing gloves, carefully fill it. Keep the tube upright and leave to cool overnight until completely hardened.
- Then, fill the 12 cm circle and the 3 savarin moulds. Leave to cool.
- Use a spoon to make 5 or 6 small discs on the silicone mat. Leave to cool for 10 minutes. Run the flame of the blowtorch over it to heat slightly. Stick half of the coarsely-crushed sugar glass on top. Set the other half aside for the assembly.
- Set aside the remaining poured sugar in a semi-liquid state to use as a sticking agent.

NOUGATINE

- Prepare the sesame seed nougatine. While it is still hot, fill the silicone mould to make a disc. Leave to cool, then unmould. Pour the remaining nougatine onto baking parchment on the work surface and roll out to a thickness of 0.5 cm. Then, use a large knife to cut four strips of nougatine 1.5 cm wide and 25 cm long and cut the ends at an angle. Curl them around the circular mould and leave overnight on a baking tray lined with baking parchment.

DAY 2
PULLED SUGAR

- Prepare the pulled sugar, then make pulled sugar ribbons (see p. 286). Heat them under a sugar lamp before shaping them into bows. You can also make sugar rings (see p. 288).

ASSEMBLY

- Using a knife, carefully cut the PVC tube to release the poured sugar.
- Unmould and place all the other elements for the artistic centrepiece on the silicone mats (3). Use the sandpaper to gently rub the edges of the pastillage pieces to round off any sharp angles (4).
- Put the gold cardboard cake board on a stable surface. Take a small piping bag of tempered chocolate and pipe a coin-sized dot on the cardboard. Place the 10 cm chocolate disc on top, then pipe another dot on top and centre the 12 cm nougatine disc on it.
- Use the tip of a knife to place a thin line of semi-liquid poured sugar on the surface of the nougatine (5). Place the 12 cm ring of chocolate on top, followed by the poured sugar tube in the centre. Leave to stand for a few minutes to ensure that the components are well bonded to each other.
- Put a line of semi-liquid poured sugar at the top of the tube and place an upside-down poured sugar savarin disc on top. Use the spirit level to ensure that the disc is straight (6).
- Fill the space between the poured sugar tube and the chocolate ring with half of the crushed poured sugar.
- Next, stick the four curved strips of nougatine around the sugar tube and attach the four curved strips of pastillage between the nougatine strips with semi-liquid poured sugar (7). Leave to stand for a few minutes to ensure that the components are well bonded to each other. Stick two more savarin discs to the top of the piece, flat sides together.
- One by one, dip the decorative elements in the semi-liquid poured sugar, then attach them to the centrepiece, starting with the larger ones: pastillage leaves and flowers and a butterfly (8). When it comes to sticking, if there are small imperfections, don't hesitate to cover them by attaching a decorative element, such as a small disc of poured sugar covered with coarsely crushed poured sugar (9).
- Follow the initial sketch as closely as possible, adding little bows of pulled sugar ribbon, pastillage and pulled sugar rings. Finish by delicately applying a few touches of gold leaf with the tip of a knife.
- This artistic centrepiece will keep for up to 3 or 4 days in a dry place, or ideally for up to 1 or 2 months under a bell jar with calcium chloride granules.

GLOSSARY

ACIDULATE
To add lemon juice or vinegar to prevent oxidation (e.g. for fruit).

BAIN-MARIE
A method of cooking or reheating which involves placing a container with a preparation in it over a saucepan of simmering water. It is used when a preparation should not be boiled directly (e.g. sabayon), or for gently melting an ingredient (e.g. chocolate).

BEAT
To whisk an ingredient (e.g. egg white, cream) or mixture to give it volume.

BLANCHING
To submerge a food (e.g. citrus fruit) into boiling water to precook, soften or remove excess bitterness.

BLOOM
A measure of the strength of gelatine, named after the American Oscar Bloom, inventor of the gelometer. The greater the strength required, the higher the Bloom of the gelatine. In addition, the higher the Bloom of a gelatine, the greater its capacity to absorb water.

BOIL
The appearance of bubbles in a hot liquid (98 to 100°C).

BITE (BOUCHÉE)
A small bite-sized morsel or confectionery that can be introduced into the mouth in a single bite. Often a coated chocolate with a filling.

CANDY
To cover a confectionery centre or preparation with a protective sugar crust by soaking it in candy syrup, then leaving it to dry.

CARAMELISE
To cook sugar for various preparations until it takes on an amber colour.

CHABLONNAGE
To spread a very thin layer of tempered chocolate or GLAZE over the base of a preparation to make it resistant.

CHOP
To cut a food or ingredient into small pieces using a knife or food processor (e.g. candied fruit, chocolate, hazelnuts, almonds).

COAT
To cover a food completely and evenly with another ingredient (e.g. chocolate, cocoa, sugar).

CONFIT
Food that has been soaked in an ingredient (e.g. sugar, alcohol) to saturation point, allowing it to be preserved.

COOKING
The action and way a food is cooked.

CUT
To slice or divide an ingredient into even-sized pieces.

CUT OUT
To use a knife, scissors or biscuit cutter to cut out specific shapes from a preparation.

DEGREE BAUMÉ
A unit of measurement for the sugar content of syrups in relation to water, i.e. the sugar content of the syrup. The most common syrup is 30° Baumé, made from a mixture of 1 litre water and 1.35 kg sugar. In 1961 it was no longer considered a legal unit in France, and it was replaced with a unit of measurement called Brix (Bx).

To calculate the degree Brix from a degree Baumé measurement, multiply the degree Baumé by 1.8 (e.g. 30° Baumé x 1.8 = 54° Brix).

DEGREE BRIX
Refractometer unit of measurement indicating the refractive index of a sugar solution. It is used to accurately measure the sugar content of a solution.

A degree Brix corresponds to the weight in grams of sugar diluted in 100 ml of pure solution. For example, a 20° Brix syrup contains 20% sugar.

DRAIN
Pour food through a sieve or colander to remove the liquid in which it has been cooked or soaked.

DRY
To remove excess water from a mixture by stirring it continuously over heat with a spatula until it comes away from the sides (e.g. prune cream).

DUST
To sprinkle a light veil of a powdered ingredient (e.g. icing sugar, starch) over a work surface in contact with the preparation (e.g. dough) to prevent it sticking.

EXTRACT
The concentrated extract of a food used to flavour a preparation (e.g. coffee extract).

FILL
To fill or stuff the inside of a food with a preparation (e.g. filled barley sugar, stuffed dates).

FLAKE
To cut nuts (e.g. almonds) lengthways into thin slices, by hand or by machine.

FOLD
To gradually incorporate one food into another, combining them very gently.

FONDANT
A preparation made with sugar, water and glucose used to glaze cakes and desserts, which is also used in many confectionery products.

FRASER
To work a dough by pushing it in front of you with the palm of your hand, to homogenise it without working it too much.

GANACHE
A mixture of cream and chocolate used, among other things, to FILL chocolates.

GAVOTTES® CRÊPES
Crushed pieces of crêpes dentelle.

GELATINE MASS
The weight of the gelatine once it has hydrated. Gelatine in powder or leaf form is hydrated, generally with 5 times its weight in water. A gelatine mass can be prepared in advance in large quantities and weighed when needed.

GLAZE
A mixture of ingredients with a syrupy consistency used to COAT a food (e.g. candied chestnuts).

GRATE
To shred into fine strips or powder using a special implement (e.g. coconut).

GRIND
To crush or pound to a more or less fine texture.

HARDEN
To set or crystallise from a liquid to a solid state (e.g. cooked sugar syrup, a chocolate coating following tempering).

INFUSE
To add an aromatic ingredient to a simmering liquid and leaving it to rest so that the aroma diffuses into the liquid (e.g. tea).

KNIFE TIP
A measure corresponding to what can be held on the tip of a knife (e.g. a knife tip of vanilla powder).

LINE
To line the sides and/or base of a mould with a sheet of baking parchment, soft acetate guitar sheet or Rhodoïd® (acetate) sheet to make it easier to unmould.

MELT
To make a solid food liquid by heating it (e.g. chocolate).

MOISTEN
Humidify with liquid.

MOULD
To fill a mould with a mixture or dough, before or after cooking.

OIL
To coat a baking tray or mould with a thin layer of oil to prevent food from sticking to it.

PEEL
To remove the skin, rind or inedible parts from a fruit or vegetable.

PINCH
A small amount of an ingredient that can be held between the thumb and forefinger (e.g. salt, sugar).

PIT
To remove the stone or pit from a fruit using a knife or pitter.

POACH
To cook an ingredient in a liquid kept at a gentle simmer (e.g. fruit in a sugar syrup).

PRALINE (1)
A confectionery invented by Clément Jaluzot (1598-1675), cook to the Marshall of France, Duke of Choiseul and Count of Plessis-Praslin. A paste made from sugar, almonds or hazelnuts, all caramelised and crushed and used to flavour or decorate.

PRALINE (2)
1. To flavour a confectionery by adding praline paste.

2. The praline-making process that involves coating almonds or hazelnuts in cooked sugar.

REDUCE
To BOIL a liquid until it has evaporated and diminished in volume. The mixture becomes thicker and the flavours more concentrated.

REFRESH
To cool food that has just been BLANCHED quickly with cold water.

GLOSSARY

ROAST
To brown nuts evenly on a baking tray in a hot oven (e.g. walnuts, almonds, pistachios).

ROLL OUT
To roll out a dough using a rolling pin to the desired thickness and size.

ROUGHLY CHOP
To coarsely chop or crush an ingredient using a knife or a mortar and pestle.

ROYAL ICING
A mixture of sugar, egg whites and lemon juice used to GLAZE pastries or decorate artistic centrepieces.

RUB IN
To rub a fat into flour to distribute it evenly. Stop as soon as it resembles fine breadcrumbs.

SEEDING
A technique for tempering chocolate by melting two thirds of a quantity of chocolate, then adding the remaining unmelted third and stirring until smooth.

SEEP
Describes a praline that has not been properly homogenised and the fat seeps from it.

SIFT OR SIEVE
To run an ingredient (e.g. cocoa, flour, icing sugar) through a sieve to make it lump-free.

SIMMER
To heat a liquid to the point before coming to the boil, when the bubbles are barely perceptible.

SLICE
To CUT an ingredient (e.g. fruit) into thin, flat even slices.

SKIM
To remove the foam that forms on the surface of a boiling liquid.

SKIN
To remove the skins from fruit (e.g. almonds, peaches, pistachios) after BLANCHING them.

SMOOTH
1. To make a firm or set preparation more supple by vigorously WHISKING it.

2. To use a spatula to even the surface of a preparation so that it is flat.

SOFTENED BUTTER
Butter that is soft but not melted.

SPRINKLE
To scatter the surface of a sweet or dessert with a powdered ingredient.

STICK/GLUE
To moisten a surface with water to join two doughs together (e.g. ravioli).

STIFFEN
To add a small amount of sugar to whisked egg whites, then WHISK a little more until firm. This makes them shiny and stops them from losing volume.

STOP THE COOKING PROCESS
To reduce or stop the cooking of a preparation (e.g. caramel, sugar syrup) by gradually adding cold or hot liquid.

STRAIN
To filter a preparation, generally through a rounded or conical sieve.

SUGAR COAT/CANDY
To put nuts in a cooked sugar syrup and stir until well coated and whitened.

SUGAR DECORATION
A preparation based on sugar and colouring agents (e.g. pulled sugar, blown sugar, spun sugar, poured sugar, pressed sugar, pastillage).

TABLING
A method of tempering couverture chocolate that is done on a marble work surface.

TEMPERING
To run chocolate through three separate temperature stages to improve its shine and give it a good snap.

Once tempered, chocolate can be poured into a mould, or used to make decorations and coat chocolates.

THICKEN
To solidify a preparation (e.g. cream or fruit compote) using a thickener (e.g. starch or pectin).

UNMOULD
To remove a culinary preparation from the mould in which it has been placed to give it a particular shape.

WHISK
To beat a preparation with a whisk to cream it, lighten it or make it frothy.

ZEST
To remove the colourful outer skin of a citrus fruit (e.g. orange, lemon). Zest can be added to a mixture to flavour it, or it can be CANDIED.

RECIPE INDEX

Recipe	Page
Almond paste	42
Almond paste figures	274
Apple sweets	156
Ardoises	184
Artistic centrepiece	302
Bergamotes from Nancy	152
Brigadeiro	236
Butterscotch	206
Calissons	144
Candied chestnuts	106
Candied orange peel	36
Candy canes	94
Candy syrup	39
Caprices	172
Chewy caramels with fine "fleur de sel" sea salt	86
Chikki	212
Chocolate buttons with hundreds and thousands	112
Chocolate-coated almonds	114
Chocolate-coated candied orange peel	110
Chocolate fondant cherries	134
Chocolate nougat	116
Chocolate praline rochers	124
Chocolate spread	82
Christmas tree	298
Coffee toffee	202
Confit chestnuts	106
Coussins de Lyon	168
Cremino	220
Crystallised rose petals	96
Crystallised violets	96
Dalgona	208
Dark chocolate sarments	182
Dark chocolate truffles	120
Dried fruit	246
Easter egg	294
Filled barley sugar	98
Filled chocolate lollipops	138
Fizzy berlingots	152
Fondant	40
Fruit crisps	246
Gianduiotto	224
Gianduja	224
Gluten-free buckwheat and coffee bites	270
Gold-flecked palettes	128
Granola bars	252
Griottines® chocolates	134
Halva	219
Hard coffee caramels	90
Hard nougat	78
Homemade chocolate bars with no white sugar	264
Lactose-free soft caramels	260
Liquid-centred sweets	102
Liquorice	64
Lokums	192
Mandarin fruit jellies	60
Mendiants	112
Menhirs	176
Milk chocolate truffles	120
Mirabelles from Lorraine	158
Moulded passion fruit chocolates	132
Mozartkugel	228
Nougatine	278
Nougatines de Nevers	164
Orange marmalade	190
Pastillage	280
Pears candied in birch sugar	244
Pink marshmallows	70
Pink pralines	148
Poured sugar	282
Praline paste	44
Pressed fruit bars	240
Pressed sugar	282
Pulled sugar	286
Ravioli sweets filled with fruit jelly	66
Reduced sugar lollipops	262
Reduced sugar pecan praline	256
Reduced sugar raspberry jam	245
Royal icing	282
Schokoküss	232
Soft nougat	74
Soft nougat with aquafaba	258
Strawberry flavoured syrup	38
Stuffed dates	214
Sugar- and lactose-free coconut and cinnamon truffles	271
Tamarind and coconut lollipops	198
Tas de sel	180
Turrón	218
Valentine's Day centrepiece	290
Vanilla fudge	202
White chocolate coconut rochers	124
Wine gums	194

ACKNOWLEDGEMENTS

It would not have been possible to create this book without the expertise, and the constant support and enthusiasm of the coordination teams. Thank you to our Pastry Chefs, including Emanuele Martelli, the teams of Chefs from Le Cordon Bleu institutes around the world, and assistants Eunchay Oh, Suci Maulani and Kathryn Tecler. Thanks to photographers Charly Deslandes and Emmanuelle Levesque, and photography assistant Léopoldine Besnard. Thank you to Jean-François Deguignet, Christian Lalonde (PhotoluxStudio) and Olivier Ploton. Thanks also to the administrative team: Leanne Mallard, Kaye Baudinette, Isaure Cointreau, Lynne Westney and Carrie Lee Brown.

Our special thanks go to Isabelle Jeuge-Maynard and Ghislaine Stora of Larousse and their entire team, Émilie Franc, Géraldine Lamy, Marion Dellapina, Frédéric Manlay, Fanny Delahaye and Émilie Laudrin.

We would like to express our sincere gratitude to the Le Cordon Bleu **Paris** institute and the Chefs Éric Briffard MOF, Patrick Caals, Williams Caussimon, Philippe Clergue, Alexandra Didier, Olivier Guyon and René Kerdranvat, Franck Poupard, Guillaume Siegler, Yann Morel, Fabrice Danniel, Laurent Bichon, Frédéric Deshayes, Corentin Droulin, Richard Lecoq, Oliver Mahut, Emanuele Martelli, Soyeon Park, Olivier Boudot and Frédéric Hoël;

To Le Cordon Bleu **London** and Chefs Emil Minev, Éric Bediat, Julie Walsh, Anthony Boyd, Colin Barnett, Jamal Bendghoughi, Marco Ardemagni, Zakaria El Hamdou, Fabrice Monperrus, Colin Westal, Jean-Francois Favy, Nick Patterson, Matthew Hodgett, Dominique Moudart, Circle Wong and Douglas Bond Mollitt;

To Le Cordon Bleu **Madrid** and Chefs Erwan Poudoulec, Yann Barraud, David Millet, Diego Muñoz, Clement Raybaud, Sonia Andrés, Benjamin Estienne, Manuel Lucas, David Vela and Natalia Vasquez;

To Le Cordon Bleu **Istanbul** and Chefs Erich Ruppen, Marc Leon Pauquet, Andreas Erni, Paul Metay and Luca De Astis;

To Le Cordon Bleu **Lebanon** and Chefs Philippe Wavrin and Joan Berton;

To Le Cordon Bleu **Ottawa** and Chefs Yannick Anton, Yann Le Coz, Vincent Koperski, Beatrice Dupasquier and Arnaud DeClerq;

To Le Cordon Bleu **Peru** and Chefs Gregor Funke, Bruno Arias, Javier Ampuero, Riders Rosini, Luis Muñoz, Luis Mendivil, Pierre Marchand, Diego Pomez, Sandro Reghellin, Luis Herrera, Daniel Punchin, Gisella Quesquen, Carolina Novi, Miguel Ballona, Martin Tufro, Anarella Alva, Samuel Moreau, Gabriela Zoia, Milenka Olarte and Angel Cardenas;

To Le Cordon Bleu **Mexico** and Chefs Thomas Stork, Aldo Omar Morales, Denis Delaval, Carlos Santos, Carlos Barrera Palacios, Edmundo Martínez, Thierry Laprune, Esther Galeana and Fernanda Díaz Laredo Tlaseca;

To Le Cordon Bleu **São Paulo** and Chefs Patrick Martin, Salvador Ariel, Alain Uzan, Paulo Soares, Juliete Soulé, Wilson Fernandes, Vitor Oliveira, Cézar Copquel, Danilo Soares and Ingrid Coimbra;

To Le Cordon Bleu **Rio de Janeiro** and Chefs Philippe Brye, Yann Kamps, Pablo Peralta, Thais Mouros, Mylene Brito, Eduardo Jacobsohn, Eduardo Ribeiro, Ozair Cavalcanti, Marcus Sales and Jonas Ferreira;

To Le Cordon Bleu **Japan** and Chef Gilles Company;

To Le Cordon Bleu **Korea** and Chefs Sébastien de Massard, Antoine Chassonnery, Roland Hinni, Pierre Legendre, Martin Ducout, Patrick Fournes, Jean Hubert Garnier and Hubert Bonnier;

To Le Cordon Bleu **Thailand** and Chefs Rodolphe Onno, David Gee, Marc Champire, Marc Razurel, Martin Rainbacher, Niruch Chotwatchara, Laurent Ganguillet, Wilairat Kornnoppaklao, Atikhun Tantrakool, Wichian Trirattanavatin, Jean Phillipe, Aurelien Trougne and Lien Chan Fai;

To Le Cordon Bleu **Shanghai** and Chefs Phillipe Groult MOF, Phillipe Labbé, Alexander stephen, Sasha Ernaus, Jérôme Rohard, Teva Canoni, Alain-Michel Caminade, Damien Ortal and Benjamin Fantini;

To Le Cordon Bleu **Taiwan** and Chefs Sebastien Graslan and Florian Guillemenot;

To Le Cordon Bleu **Malaysia** and Chefs Stéphane Frelon, Sylvain Dubreau, Sarju Ranavaya, Thierry Lerallu, Frederic Oger and Julien Bartement;

To Le Cordon Bleu **New Zealand** and Chefs Sébastien Lambert, Francis Motta, Evan Michelson, Sam Heeney, Paul Dicken, Nicolas Longayrou and Vincent Boudet;

And to the Le Cordon Bleu **India**, **Australia**, **Chile** and **Manila** teams.

This English language edition published in 2024 by
Grub Street
4 Rainham Close
London
SW11 6SS

Email: food@grubstreet.co.uk
Web: www.grubstreet.co.uk
Twitter/X: @grub_street
Facebook: Grub Street Publishing
Instagram: grubstreetpublishinguk

Copyright this English language edition © Grub Street 2024
Copyright © Larousse 2023
Copyright for the text © Le Cordon Bleu International BV
Published originally in French as Le Cordon Bleu *L'École de la Confiserie*

Recipe photography and presentation: © Charly Deslandes
Recipe styling and step-by-step photographs:
© Emmanuelle Levesque, assisted by Léopoldine Besnard
Photographs on pages 4, 5, 7, 15, 18, 20, 21: © Le Cordon Bleu
Photographs on pages 42, 44, 45, 46, 47, 49, 50, 51, 53, 54, 55, 57:
© Olivier Ploton
Photograph on page 208: © Shutterstock

A CIP catalogue record for this book is available from the British Library.

ISBN 978-1-911714-17-0

The moral right of the author has been asserted.

All rights reserved. Without limiting the rights under copyright reserved above, no part of this publication may be reproduced, stored in or introduced into a retrieval system, or transmitted, in any form or by any means (electronic, mechanical, photocopying, recording or otherwise) without the prior written permission of both the copyright owner and the above publisher of this book.

Printed and bound in Czechia by Finidr